2 GLASGOW CENTRES | 1 MEMBERSHIP

THE PROP STORE IS A WELCOMING CLIMBING CENTRE IN MARYHILL | CAFE | COURSES + COACHING | BOULDERING | ROPED CLIMBING | AUTO BELAY | GYM | COMPS | TRAINING FACILITIES | FREE PARKING | KIDS CLASSES

THECLIMBINGACADEMY.COM

THE CLIMBING ACADEMY

ISBN 978-0-9928876-2-9

A CIP catalogue record for this book is available from the British Library.
Published by Stone Country Press Ltd., 61 Sinclair Drive, Glasgow, G42 9PU
www.stonecountrypress.co.uk

DISCLAIMER

Rock climbing can be a dangerous sport that can lead to serious injury or risk of fatality. You should not undertake the routes described in this guide without proper experience, training or equipment. By using this guide you acknowledge that the information therein may be out of date or inaccurate and you agree that the publisher cannot be held liable for any damage or injury that may be caused when climbing the routes in this guide. Climbers must accept responsibility for judging a route before climbing it. The contents of this guide have been checked to be as accurately described as possible at the date of publication. The publisher cannot be held responsible for any omissions or mistakes, nor liable for any personal or third party injuries. It is recommended that climbers obtain suitable insurance and assume all responsibility for their climbing.

Photo: Dumbarton drone's eye view © Chris Houston

THE CLIMBER'S COMPLETE GUIDE TO

DUMBARTON ROCK

J.S. WATSON & JOHN HUTCHINSON

CONTENTS

Hamish Potokar on the 'Chahala link project' © Sam Scriven

PREFACE

Dumbarton Rock, 'The Rock', or just 'Dumby' to climbers – this volcanic plug is one of Scotland's most impressive and unique climbing venues.

Concentrated on the overhanging north-west aspects and around a cluster of huge boulders below, there are hundreds of top-quality problems and many excellent trad and sport routes. Located within convenient and easy reach of Glasgow and the Central Belt, Dumby offers an escape from the bustle of the city without really having to leave it at all.

Dumby's routes and boulder problems have a reputation for being hard and unforgiving. This is due to the notorious lack of friction on its smooth basalt, which requires precise technique and athletic power to unlock. On first acquaintance many are put off by the physical and mental demands placed on them – the often insecure and marginal nature of the climbing a world away from the readability of indoor walls with coloured, grippy holds. Dedication and perseverance are key to adapting to Dumby's unique climbing style, and for those that do return a lifetime of rewarding climbing awaits. There are also plenty of easier climbs to enjoy, where beginners can get their first taste of real rock and begin a climbing apprenticeship that travels well.

Dumby is a pleasant place to hang out during the summer, particularly in the long daylight hours of the evening when many descend upon the Rock after work. There's nothing quite like a circuit of the classic problems under a spectacular Dumby sunset to hit the reset button and clear the mind. Indeed, its reputation as a 'hardman crag' often obscures its more pleasant and amenable qualities, especially in the bouldering – it's a place that softens with the knowing. There are as many easy problems as hard problems and plenty for all ages and abilities if you find the routes too intimidating. This history and guide will help give you the information and inspiration to build your attachment to this wonderful climbing resource.

We hope you too discover some of that Dumby magic!

John Hutchinson & John Watson

The hard whinstone, which here rises up abruptly from the alluvial shores of the River Clyde, exhibits in a very interesting and beautiful manner the crystalline arid prismatic structure peculiar to such trappean effusions, but the lines of fracture or divisional planes of the Rock of Dumbarton are observed to incline generally at an angle of about 70° giving to the Rock on one of its sides a rather precipitous and overhanging appearance.

Capt. L. Brickenden, Journal of the Geological Society, 1855

Dumbarton Rock looking east © Stewart Brown

ROCK OF AGES – A BRIEF HISTORY

Due to its strategic location at the confluence of the River Leven and the River Clyde, Dumbarton Rock's recorded history stretches back 1,500 years, with human settlement likely as far back as the Iron Age. A twin-topped dome of basalt, the Rock consists of an eastern peak with a broad, level summit of 69m (The Beak) and a more rugged western peak that rises to a height of 74m (White Tower Crag) separated from one another by a deep, central gully. The Rock makes its first appearance in recorded history around AD 450, with early literary references made to 'Altclut', a British name meaning 'rock of the Clyde'. For over 500 years, the powerful British kingdom of Strathclyde was ruled from Dumbarton Rock, a history reflected in the etymology of the place name Dumbarton – derived from the Scottish Gaelic 'Dun Breatann', meaning 'the fortress of the Britons'. Despite its formidable natural defences, the Rock was successfully raided by Vikings in AD 870, led by Olaf the White, King of Dublin, and Ivar 'the Boneless', after a four-month siege. Despite such a catastrophic setback, the kingdom of Strathclyde gradually re-emerged in the 10th century, its kings ruling over a vast territory that extended north of Loch Lomond to as far south as Cumbria. Eventually, Strathclyde would be absorbed into a united Scotland in 1034, a merger engendered when King Duncan of Strathclyde ascended to the Scottish throne as Duncan I.

Because of its strategic importance in controlling shipping and trade along the Firth of Clyde, Dumbarton Rock's defensive position was to be continually utilised throughout the ensuing centuries, often changing hands between rivals. Acting as an important medieval royal castle and military staging point, it was embroiled in the tumultuous events of the Wars of Independence, with William Wallace reputedly held prisoner within its walls in 1305. In 1489 James IV captured the castle from its rebellious keeper John Stewart, Earl of Lennox (with the help of his famous cannon Mons Meg) and subsequently used it as a military staging point from which he led many expeditions against the dissenting Lords of the Isles. This turned the town of Dumbarton into a bustling naval base, with ships being built, repaired and provisioned there – a shipbuilding role that would be fully realised in the Clydeside shipyards of the nineteenth and twentieth centuries. In the sixteenth century, an infant Mary Queen of Scots found refuge behind the castle's walls before being conveyed to France. In the civil war that followed Mary on her return to the country as an adult, the castle was captured from the 'Queen's Party'

Neil Macniven and Brian Shields on 'Chemin de Fer', 1963

for her rival James VI on the early morning of 1 April 1571. Led by Captain Thomas Crawford of Jordanhill, approximately 100 men made a daring ascent of the north-east side of *The Beak* and caught the garrison unawares, establishing the Rock's first recorded climb. This operation wasn't without its complications, however, as Ken Crocket's 1975 Western Outcrops guidebook describes: 'several of the party fell off when ladders collapsed and one man was seized with a fit and was consequently tied to the ladder and used as a rung'. Despite these difficulties, Crawford and his party reached the castle ramparts around dawn (their stealth aided by a morning fog) and quickly wrested the castle from its unexpecting occupants. According to historical records, the attackers were helped by the fact that around 25 of the castle garrison were 'whoring and drinking' in the town. Crawford's ascent of 'The Beike' was playfully graded Very Severe & A1 in Ken Crocket's 1975 guide – not bad for a route nearly 500 years old.

Although the strategic importance of the castle waned as the technology of warfare changed, it continued to serve as a state prison and garrisoned fortress throughout the Napoleonic Wars, with most of its extant fortifications originating in this period. Throughout the nineteenth century the castle also became a popular tourist attraction, with famous visitors including Dorothy and William Wordsworth and Samuel Taylor Coleridge in 1803, and Queen Victoria on HMY *The Fairy* in 1847. Despite this transition from military stronghold to monument, the Rock would be called into action once more, when an anti-aircraft battery was mounted on its ramparts during the Second World War to protect the high density of shipyards and industry at its base. On the night of the 5-6th May 1941, four high-explosive bombs landed on the Rock, likely intended for the Blackburn aircraft factory and Denny's shipyard located adjacent to its northern aspect. This enemy attack was the first on the stronghold since it had fallen to Oliver Cromwell in 1652, and the last in its recorded history. In 1909 the castle and its grounds were taken into the care of the Office of Works, including the rock faces and most of the boulders, with the site declared an Ancient Scheduled Monument of National Importance in 1994.

One of the many quirks of climbing at the Rock is the long history of the castle above and its status as an Ancient Scheduled Monument. Indeed, in an early guide to the Rock (*The Glasgow Outcrops*, 1975) some of the recommended belay points are from the castle's many cannons, which of course is no longer advised! Despite the successive waves of human history that have crashed at its base, the Rock has remained, unchanging and resolute – a tangible, material connection to the past. It's safe to say that people have loitered around its boulders and rock faces long before the emergence of rock climbers, evidenced by the myriad historic graffiti and etchings that adorn its dark basalt canvas.

In the pre- and post-war periods the area around Dumbarton Rock was effectively an industrial complex, with the famous William Denny and Brothers shipyard located at its base (where the renowned clipper *Cutty Sark* was built), and Ballantine's whisky distillery across the Leven (for so long an iconic red-brick tower in the climbing background, demolished in early 2017). Like the rest of the Firth of Clyde, most of these industries have since disappeared, leaving behind the empty and abandoned spaces of post-industrial decline. This 'wasteland' aesthetic has contributed to the somewhat urban and edgy reputation of Dumby, with its stark surroundings seemingly an extension of its hard and unforgiving climbing. In recent years there has been a concentrated effort to improve the locale around the Rock to provide a more civil and recreational

Brian Shields on 'Windjammer' © Brian Shields

Ken Crocket on an early aid ascent of 'Requiem', 1974
© Ken Crocket

environment that is more connected to the town centre, though the expansion of adjacent housing developments seems to be the main priority thus far. Thankfully, the Rock's status as an Ancient Scheduled Monument means that climbing at the Rock should remain undisturbed in the coming decades, despite development pressures around it. In a 2015 statement of significance, the Rock's owners (Historic Environment Scotland) officially recognised the importance of its climbing heritage:

> 'The Rock itself has a particular importance for the climbing and bouldering community and is a celebrated venue for this sport, which has grown significantly in importance over recent decades … There is a strong sense of community amongst the climbers here which is founded on shared practice and appreciation of place rather than residence. The Dumby website and social media create an even greater sense of cohesion among this group which is expressed as deep feelings of attachment and affection for the place in all its moods …'

Dumbarton Rock's climbing scene is centred around its steep, imposing north-west face and huge boulders below. Calved from the main crag in the post-glacial period around 10,000 years ago, the Rock's monolithic blocs have provided shelter and a place to hang out ever since. Although the early pioneers of rock climbing in Scotland were aware of the impressive crags and boulders below Dumbarton Castle, there is no recorded history of climbing there until 1963. On first impression, it seems quite surprising that it took climbers until the early 1960s to realise there was such a gem on the doorstep of the Central Belt, but in reality, the climbing was too futuristic for the standards and equipment of the time. There were also cultural reasons too, whereby lowland crags were considered only as a source of amusement and practice for the 'real climbing' to be had in the mountains. Despite this historical apathy, in the 1960s something of a cultural renaissance occurred at the Rock as climbers began to realise its potential for new routing and, perhaps a little surprisingly, bouldering. In the first-ever climbing guide to the Rock, handwritten circa 1964 in a 'Winfield' notebook by the pioneering Brian Shields, he writes:

> 'As a rock climbing practice ground, Dumbarton Rock has been sadly neglected, and it is only in the last year that routes and boulder problems have been opened up. There are over twenty routes on the face, and over fifty boulder problems, which although often

Brian Shields on 'Pendulum' in the 60s © Brian Shields

ridiculously short present the climber with a pleasant evening's climbing, and the difficulty of many is formidable.'

It was the emergence of specialised rock boots from Europe during this time that allowed climbers to begin to get a conceptual and physical foothold on the compact basalt of Dumbarton Rock. At the vanguard of these pioneers were the talented young duo of Brian Shields and Neil Macniven. Focusing on the Rock's obvious cracks and corner lines, in 1963 they established routes such as *Stonefall Crack* (HVS) and the aid route *Chemin de Fer* (A2). They also recognised the potential of the Rock's boulders for testing both technical skill and mental control, putting up the bold 'route-style' problems of *B.N.I.* (E1 5c), *Route Royale* (E3 5c), *Sucker's Slab* (Brit 5b) and *The Switch* (Brit 5a). While laying these foundations of the bold Dumbarton climbing style, Macniven and Shields were also testing their strength on the steep, hard starts of *Nemesis* and *Pas Encore* at the grades of British 5b and 5c respectively. Compiled from the handwritten guide of Shields, the many new routes established through his fruitful partnership with Macniven were first published in the SMC Journal of 1965, though the Rock's 50+ boulder problems were omitted. Interestingly, it appears that the Rock's reputation for danger and seriousness was apparent even from the start. In a letter from the prominent post-war climber Jimmy Marshall to Shields, in which he describes the details of his first-ascent of *Grasshopper* (E2 5c) on the Etive Slabs, Marshall writes: '. . . would think this is very small potatoes compared to Dumbarton Rock and its very frightening looking problems!'

Aid climbing was also practised at this time on the boulders, including the overhanging crack of the modern-day boulder problem *Pongo*, which Shields describes in his original guide: 'Just left of *Sorcerer's Slab*, on the overhanging wall, a thin crack can be seen. Climb it, using five pegs. The pegs tend to bounce out, but the grass is reasonable to land on.' If you look carefully, old peg scars remain in *Pongo* as well as in the *Good Nicks* crack. Other material traces of this era are evident in the faint arrows etched into the boulders by Shields in the 1960s to indicate the starting point of various problems. In 1964, Macniven was tragically killed in the Alps at the age of 21. Despite the loss of his friend and climbing partner, Shields carried on new-routing at the Rock throughout the remainder of the decade with Michael 'Silver' Connolly and others, establishing *Windjammer Crack* (with only two wooden wedges for protection) as well as the aid lines of *Longbow* (A3), *The Big Zipper* (A3) and further boulder problems such as *Short Notice* (Brit 5b) and *Skint Knuckles* (Brit 5b). Perhaps the most remarkable ascent was a midwinter A4 aid-climbing assault on *Requiem* in December 1964. Shields described this route in his guide: 'The "last great problem" of Dumbarton Rock – the centre crack of the North Face overhang. Climb up the first few pegs of *Chemin de Fer* and traverse diagonally right on pegs and expansion bolts to the foot of the centre crack, which climbs on pegs and wedges until it peters out; then use expansion bolts to reach the top of the face. The route is climbed in one run-out. The traverse-flake is dangerously loose, and could certainly 'unzip' if the first peg in the main crack were to come out. Exposure in extreme.'

In the late 60s and early 70s, a new crop of 'Dumbarton Boys' emerged at the Rock, including Rab Carrington, John Jackson and the duo of 'Big' Ian Nicolson and 'Wee' Ian Fulton. This new generation brought a Glasgow swagger to the Rock, and alongside a clutch of often bold new routes, they established newer and harder boulder problems, some of which took weeks to work out – the era of 'the project' had arrived. The audacious attitude of this 1970s generation is encapsulated well by the

Dave Cuthbertson on the first free ascent of 'Chemin de Fer' © Ken Johnstone

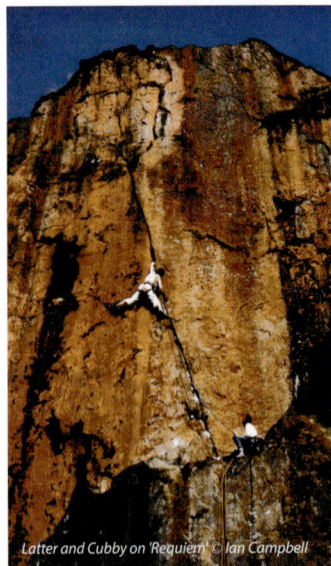

Latter and Cubby on 'Requiem' © Ian Campbell

Latter on 'Big Zipper Direct' © Gary Latter

exploits of Ian Nicolson, a Creagh Dhu legend, who stamped his name in Dumby folklore after a solo ascent of *Stonefall Crack*, allegedly with a broken arm in plaster! Other new routes were established throughout the 1970s on the Rock's North Face and Gully Wall, filling in the gaps left from the 1960s. Being far less pleasing in aspect than the spectacular North West Face around the corner, and with no easy anchor points, both sectors are now long-neglected and overgrown.

In the early 1970s a visiting gritstone climber, Steve Belk, made the first free ascent of Shields' *Longbow*, as well as a bold lead of the *Requiem* headwall on tied-off blade pegs, relinquishing the expansion bolts utilised by Shields. Belk's partner on the day, Ken Crocket, would return to *Requiem* for his own aid ascent in 1975, ending rather memorably in a ground fall for both he and his belayer! Thankfully Crocket walked away with no more than bruises and nettle stings and a great story to tell, though his belayer is now minus a spleen. Ken Johnstone was also busy during this period, adding *Slainte* (E2 5c), *Drizzle* (HVS 5a), *Crackerjack* (E1 5b), *Rough Sea* (E2 5b), and the aesthetic crack of *Antigrav* (using two points of aid and later freed by Willie Todd at E3 6a). In 1978, alongside the first ascents of routes such as *Snowwhite* (E2 5b) and *Gaucho* (E2 5c), Willie Todd brought his strong fingers to bear on *Good Nicks*, establishing the Rock's first British 6a boulder problem with a typically Dumbartonian highball finish. In the same year, emboldened by the greater technical performance of 'EB' climbing shoes, Mark Worsley climbed the committing highball crack of *Supinator* (Brit 6a), and Pete Greenwell deployed precise footwork, power, and dynamism to establish the brilliant *Gorilla* – the first to breach the technical grade of British 6b and perhaps the first truly 'modern' Dumbarton test piece. All pretty impressive considering the absence of bouldering mats and abundance of bell-bottoms! The 1970s also saw Shields establish his last route at the Rock in the form of *Resurrection* in 1974, an aid line up the right-hand corner crack of the main face (now known as *Cyclops*). Signalling the end of an era, Shields, alongside Macniven and their 1960s cohort, can be considered as the bold and exploratory early pioneers of Dumbarton rock climbing, breaking new ground and laying the cultural foundations upon which climbing generations have successively built. After a lifetime of measured risk-taking and in the words of his son Jon, 'a casual indifference to dangerous situations', Shields died in 2011 at the age of 67, leaving an astonishing legacy of climbs at Dumbarton Rock.

Like the hard graft inherent to its industrial surroundings, the Rock was proving to be a true forcing ground for Scottish rock climbing, with the freeing of the remaining major aid lines of the 1960s and 70s providing the main focus for the 1980s new wave. The main protagonists during this decade were the spritely, sinewy figures of Dave 'Cubby' Cuthbertson and Gary Latter. In the spring of 1980 Cuthbertson added *Woops* (E4 6a) and then went on to free the neighbouring *Chemin de Fer* (E5 6a) over the course of several evenings, with ropes and runners left in situ overnight. Almost 40 years later, *Chemin de Fer* remains as pumpy as ever and a significant challenge for E5 leaders, illustrating the cutting-edge and futuristic nature of Cubby's first free ascent. Cuthbertson was no slouch on the boulders either, adding the powerful and athletic *Mugsy,* the Rock's first British 6c (Font 7a), which no doubt provided useful training for the hard moves required to free the aid routes looming above. Meanwhile, Latter added the classic and varied boulder problems of *Mestizo, Toto, Physical Graffiti* and *Pongo*. All remain absolute must-dos for any aspiring Dumbarton boulderer, requiring power, precision and belief in equal measure.

Cuthbertson returned in May 1982 to free Shields' 1974 aid route *Resurrection* to establish the hard corner of *Cyclops* (E5 6b), taking numerous falls on to a pre-placed peg runner which remains to this day. In 1983, Latter climbed the bold, rising traverse of *Rock of Ages* (E3 6a) and liberated *The Big Zipper* of its two remaining aid bolts, taking six days work across the summer. As noted, at this time *The Big Zipper* was climbed direct at E4 6c (via the now-bolted *Omerta* crack), as opposed to traversing in left from *Stonefall Crack* as it is now commonly done (at E3 5b). During the same period, Cuthbertson was engaged in a protracted battle with *Requiem*, the biggest and best un-freed line of them all, cutting straight up the centre of the Rock's headline act – the North West Face. Having approached the route ground-up and fallen from the final move a number of times, an exasperated Cuthbertson decided to change tactics and rehearse the offending move on top rope. Pre-armed with the requisite muscle memory, Cuthbertson latched the final dyno move on his next lead attempt to gain the top of the headwall, and in doing so established one of the hardest lines in the UK at the time, at E7 7a (now considered E8 6c with an equivalent sports grade of around F8a+). Originally aid-climbed by Brian Shields and Michael Connolly in December 1964, Cuthbertson's first free ascent 20 years later remains one of the most iconic events in the Rock's climbing (and folk) history, as well as something of a watershed moment for Cubby himself: 'By doing *Requiem* I suddenly realised I could adapt this whole level of difficulty to all sorts of different places.'

If the 1980s were largely characterized by the freeing of old aid routes, the 1990s saw bouldering and sport climbing come of age at Dumbarton

Andy Gallagher: Dumby pioneer © Tim Morozzo

Rock, spurred on by the talent of a strong Glaswegian panel-beater named Andy Gallagher. Having served his apprenticeship at the Rock in the 1980s, between 1990 and 1994 Gallagher utilised his dynamic style to fill in many of the obvious gaps on the boulders and establish a plethora of modern classics As well as the straight-up power-problems of *Head Butt* (7a) and *Slap Happy* (7a) – possibly the most frequently failed on problem at Dumby – Gallagher also put up a new breed of sustained stamina-problems, adding a pumpy cave-lip traverse into *Mestizo* and *Mugsy* (both 7b), as well as establishing *1990 Traverse* (7b) and the intricate, super-classic low traverse of *Consolidated* (7b+). Gallagher also continued the tradition of bold, committing highballs at Dumby, breaching the foreboding black cave of the Eagle Boulder to establish *Shadow* (E6 6c, Font 7a) and *Trick of the Vale* (E7 6c, Font 7a+). The weighty E-grades attached to these problems reflect the fact that Gallagher established them ground-up, prior to the ubiquitous use of bouldering pads, with the crux apex mantle of *Trick of the Vale* providing him with a particularly memorable 'oh shit' moment during its first ascent, leading to its original grade of E7. Reflecting on his significant contribution to the Rock's modern climbing development, Gallagher cites the strange 'draw' of the place, familiar to its many devotees: 'It's one of those places that just gets right into your soul and your heart, and slowly but surely it keeps pulling you there, and pulling you there, and you're back.'

During this same 90s period a wider and sometimes uneasy culture

A young Dave MacLeod repeating 'The Shield' © Guy Robertson

'Pete Whillance on 'Gorilla' 1978 © Ken Johnstone

'Cubby on Eagle Boulder 1983 © Gary Latter

change saw bolts appear at Dumbarton Rock, opening up new climbing potential on its otherwise unprotectable, blank faces. Initially, the appearance of bolts at the Rock provoked the ire of Historic Scotland, who saw them as vandalism of an Ancient Scheduled Monument. Their response was to ban climbing from the Rock and have the bolts removed, despite the irony that this removal required further bolts to be drilled by the contracted steeplejacks. Clearly, there was a gulf in understanding at the time between the Rock's stewards and its climbing community. Thankfully, after consultation with the Mountaineering Council of Scotland (who were initially opposed to bolting at the Rock), this cultural misunderstanding was subsequently resolved and Historic Scotland resumed their position of benign indifference to the Rock's climbing scene, with bolts being drilled again from 1993 onwards.

Adding a new kind of industry to a rapidly declining Clydeside, Andy Gallagher was at the forefront of the Rock's sporting development, alongside Cameron Phair (*Half Breed* F7b, 1993), Mark 'Face' McGowan (*Tarrier* F8a, 1993) and Benny McLaughlan (*Appliance of Violence* F7b+, 1993), drilling and bolting the blank walls between the trad routes to create some modern test pieces. Gallagher bolted and climbed most of the now-classic sport lines such as *Persistence of Vision* (F7a+, 1997), *Unforgiven* (F7b, 1993) and the stunning arête of *Omerta* (F7c, 1993). The technical leaning wall right of the corner crack of *Cyclops* yielded some of the best sport routes, with the fine trio of *Dum Dum Boys* (F8a, 1995), *Sufferance* (F8a, 1993) and McGowan's *Tarrier* (F8a, 1993), as well as a number of subsequent link-ups and variations. Gallagher also displayed a keen prescience of future climbing standards by bolting the absurdly blank faces either side of the *Requiem* crack. To date only the left-hand line has been partially climbed by Alan Cassidy (lowering off at about two thirds height), to give the desperate and brilliantly named *Unfinished Symphony* (F8b+, 2013). Ascents of the full piece and its unclimbed neighbour to the right of the *Requiem* crack will both likely weigh in at around F9b!

Despite Andy Gallagher's frequent presence among the boulders, in 1994, a young and freakishly strong Malcolm Smith forayed west from his home in Dunbar to nab the first ascent of *The Shield*, the first British 7a at the Rock and genuine Font 7b+ straight-up, as well as the fierce *B.N.I. Direct* at the same grade. Gallagher described Smith as 'on another level' and Dumby would prove to be the perfect testing ground for Smith's indoor-honed power and total dedication to training, with its lack of conventional 'scenic' aesthetics more than made up for by the sheer quality and desperate nature of its unclimbed lines. In 1998 Smith duly turned up and dispatched the sit start to the *Pongo* crack in a day, climbing its full length with long, powerful lock-off moves to establish Dumby's first Font 8a. Smith's ascent of *Pongo Sit Start* brought the Rock into line with the continental standards of the time and also continued Dumby's traditional role as the laboratory of hard Scottish rock climbing.

Just as Smith was upping the bar, a pony-tailed youngster called Dave MacLeod became a constant presence at Dumbarton. Largely disinterested in the passive and didactic classroom education on offer at high school, MacLeod utilised the Rock for a self-education which would propel him to the highest levels of climbing ability and achievement.

Over ten years between 1996 and 2006, MacLeod systematically assessed the hardest projects the Rock had left to offer, dispatching them one by one through a tenacious and dedicated approach. Relocating himself to Dumbarton to be closer to his projects, 'Dumby Dave' became a perpetual, talismanic presence at the Rock as if an embodied extension of the basalt itself. Having exhausted the Rock's established lines, in 1998 Dave began to seek out his own bouldering nirvana, adding the desperate *In Bloom,* a tenuous Font 7c+ power-traverse along the poor handrail that leads into the *Pongo* crack. In 2001 he took a direct line up the *Gorilla* arête to produce the burly and aptly named *Silverback* (7c) which he then extended further the following year to establish *King Kong* (8a) – a long and arduous journey linking *Neil's Extension* (7b) into *Silverback* (7c) to finish up *Gorilla Warfare* (7a+). Unrelenting, Dave continued to push the grades on the steep overhang of the B.N.I. boulder with *Sabotage* (8a) in 2003, which was soon followed by *The Perfect Crime* (8a+). Perhaps the prime example of Dave's attritional approach, however, was his ascent of *Pressure* (8b) in 2005, taking a line through the desperate, horizontal terrain of the black cave of the Eagle Boulder – the apex of an epic siege across 100 days and four years. Deemed impossible by many strong boulderers, Dave invoked the spirit of Andy Dufresne in the film *The Shawshank Redemption* to understand that all it takes, really, is pressure and time.

Having breached these new standards, Dave went on to add a clutch of other futuristic and weighty problems such as *Sanction* (8b), *Chahala Sit Start* (8b) and the long roof problem of *Sosho* (8a+). As well as these headline acts, Dave also established an array of easier (though by no means easy) problems during his sustained tenure at the Rock, many of which have seen few or no repeats due to their often technical and committing nature, such as the aptly named *Nadjilation* (6c+ or E6 6b without mats). Dave wasn't alone in mining the Rock's hard bouldering potential however, with Malcolm Smith keeping pace deep into the new

Dave MacLeod on 'Pongo Sit Start'

Si Smith on 'Sabotage'

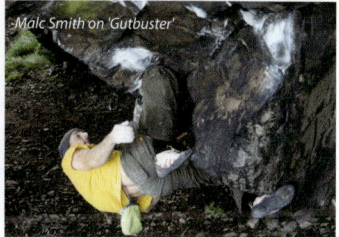

Malc Smith on 'Gutbuster'

millennium. As well as swift repeats of Macleod's matrix of test pieces, Smith emblazoned his own brand of bouldering desperation on the Rock, establishing sustained link-ups such as *Supersize Me* (8b, 2005), *Serum of Sisyphus* (8a+, 2006), the almighty *Gutbuster* (8b+, 2009), *Firefight* (8b, 2010) and *Grande Tour* (8b, 2010) – as these numbers suggest, a Font 8c remains tantalisingly close at the Rock. Perhaps of all the boulderers to inhabit Dumby, 'Malc' was always a leading presence through the 90s and into the modern 'campus-board' generation, inconspicuously visiting Dumby to dispatch his imaginative and brutal test pieces while quietly setting the bar for the next generation. His ascents echo the core character of Dumby, where a persistence of vision brings answers to the physicality and esoteric sequences of the Rock.

The early 2000s also saw several ground-breaking sport and trad first ascents. In 2003, MacLeod added *Tolerance*, Dumby's first F8b sport route via a link-up of *Tarrier*, *Sufferance* and *Dum Dum Boys*, and in 2004 he added the short power route of *Negative Creep* (F8b). On the trad front, MacLeod displayed his impressive ability to pick out unclimbed lines with a series of bold and rarely repeated routes, in the form of *Dumb and Dumber* (E7 6c, 1999), *Eh Gringo* (E4 5c, 2003), *Calm Before the Storm* (E6 6c, 2003) and *Blackout* (E6 6a, 2003). Though these routes have since fallen by the wayside somewhat, MacLeod's hard variations on the classic lines of *Chemin de Fer* and *Requiem* remain front and centre in the cultural memory of the Rock's climbing community. In 2001, MacLeod took a direct line up the headwall where the crack of *Chemin de Fer* veers left,

Hotaches filmwork of 'E11', the film that accompanied 'Rhapsody'

leaving behind the last opportunity for gear placements. The result (after 11 long falls from the desperately smooth headwall) was *Achemine* (E9 6c), Scotland's first at this grade. At an equivalent sport grade of F8b and above a huge runout, it is little surprise that to date *Achemine* has seen only one repeat, from visiting climber Barbara Zangerl in 2017. Utilising the same ethos that inspired *Achemine*, from 2004-2006 MacLeod worked the line of greatest resistance on the crown of the headwall above the *Requiem* crack – an indirect line which vaguely resembles an inverted question mark. Having eventually linked the moves on top rope, MacLeod then faced the prospect of leading F8c+ climbing above a serious runout, uttering the immortal line 'Aw no! Now I've got to fuckin' lead it!'. After a protracted and intense battle, including numerous whippers after falling from the final moves, in April 2006 MacLeod established *Rhapsody*, at the unprecedented grade of E11 7a, clocking in around seventy days of effort over two years. MacLeod justified the grade as a logical reflection of its significant fall potential and F8c+ difficulty – a technical grade that far outweighed any of the UK E10s that MacLeod had diligently repeated in preparation.

In effect, *Rhapsody* put MacLeod, and by association Dumby, on the map of the world's climbing elite, helped in large part by the Hot Aches film 'E11' which documented MacLeod's pained struggles and eventual success on the route. Drawn to the world-class challenge that *Rhapsody* offered, it saw a second ascent by the likeable Canadian crack master Sonnie Trotter in June 2008, after 24 redpoint attempts and a month of effort, eagerly followed by climbers worldwide via Trotter's blog. During this time, Trotter also added a slightly more direct solution up the headwall in the form of *DiRequiem* (E10 7a/5.14a R) and *Cop Out* (5.13b/c R – another variation which diverts to the arête earlier, missing out the crux moves of *Rhapsody*). If that wasn't enough, Trotter also repeated *Rhapsody* while placing all the gear on lead for extra style points and a 'cleaner' ascent.

A week after Trotter's *Rhapsody* saga came to an end, Steve McClure deployed his outstanding sport climbing ability to make a quick third ascent. The subsequent minor controversy that McClure had not climbed the 'true line' of *Rhapsody* (by utilising the headwall arête), highlighted the ultimately eliminate nature of its line, which for some denigrated its status and flew in the face of the UK trad ethic of the 'pure line'. The headline grade of E11 also attracted criticism, as, despite the extreme technical difficulty of *Rhapsody*, it was deemed 'safe' (mainly from the comfort of armchairs) and thus undeserving of its unprecedented E grade. More than anything though, the consternation around *Rhapsody* highlighted the unsuitability of the UK grading system (based on an onsight attempt) to cope with a trad route so technically difficult, whereby a successful ascent requires divergence from the onsight ethic that still largely defines UK trad climbing. In this sense, it is perhaps better represented by the Yosemite grading of 5.14c R (with the R denoting the high potential for a long but ultimately 'safe' fall). Such grumbles and mutterings over style, ethics and grades at the cutting edge are nothing new in climbing, and while these have long since died off, the raw challenge that *Rhapsody* offers has stood the test of time. Indeed, James Pearson, who after initially dismissing the route as contrived in 2008, returned older, wiser and stronger to climb it in 2014. It would then wait another three years for its fifth ascensionist in the form of Jacopo Larcher in 2017. It remains the jewel in the crown of Dumbarton Rock's climbing treasures and will likely remain so for years to come. An onsight ascent remains a futuristic prospect. As MacLeod's crowning achievement at the Rock, Rhapsody provided a natural stepping-off point for his pursuit of new climbing challenges elsewhere. In 2007, he duly relocated to the Highlands to be closer to a whole new series of hard projects, and 'Dumby Dave' became 'Dave MacLeod' again. In a blog post from 2007, MacLeod offers some interesting reflections on his time at the Rock:

'I am jealous of the future teenage Glaswegian climbers who discover the rock and get hooked – they have a good challenge these days to repeat the progression in grades that all the previous generations did. When I started, *Consolidated* was the hardest problem and now we do laps for the warm-up. They will have to do the same on *Sanction*! Cool. Most young climbers set their sights on or within the present limit of the day. But some look higher from the outset and decide to make it happen. Andy Gallagher, Cubby and Malcolm Smith all did that. I'll be well psyched to see the next person who takes it on … Sometime I'd also love to see everyone who lives in Dumbarton (if not Scotland) know about the value of the cliff and boulders there. The castle on top of the volcano is Dumbarton's wee claim tae fame. But that will always be something that was only important in the past – the climbing is important in the past, present and future, which is much more valuable.'

After approximately 60 years of climbing endeavours at Dumby, one might be forgiven for thinking the place was totally climbed out. However, even in the post-MacLeod years, the Rock has continued to produce quality new lines. In 2009, Will Atkinson brought a playful and energetic style to bouldering at the Rock to establish *Mr Tickle* (8a), an unlikely but superb dyno to the finishing holds of *Pongo*, and in 2019, Hamish Potokar added a sit start to *Shin Sekai* to produce *Nature* (8a+). The linking-up of existing problems has also proved fruitful, particularly on and around the 'Mugsy face' of the Home Rule boulder, with Will Atkinson's *Nice and Sleazy* (7c+, 2010), Alex Gorham's *Thoroughbred* (7c+, 2010) and Euan McFadyen's *Malky's Sleazy Chicken* (8a, 2015) being a few among many. On the sport front, Alan Cassidy climbed two-thirds of the bolted line up the blank face left of *Requiem* to establish *Unfinished Symphony* (F8b+).

Although new routing at Dumby has inevitably slowed down after 60 years at the cutting edge, it continues to provide a first-class proving ground for new generations of climbers to test their mettle, engendering fresh scenes and cooperative passions. Despite the indoor-honed power of many of the new 'young team', the challenge offered by the Rock's plethora of hard climbing remains considerable, with its unforgiving and demanding basalt a far cry from the brightly coloured security of indoor climbing holds. Thankfully though, a characterful, vigorous and gregarious community of climbers orbits the Rock, with old hands happy to dispense beta and tips to the less experienced.

The thumbnail history offered above has by necessity focused on a selection of key generational figures and first ascensionists, but the importance of the many climbers which composed their respective 'scenes' must not be overlooked. Though climbing history is recorded in the written word via guidebooks, much of it is more intangible – passed down orally in the telling of stories, 'performed' live, or through social media videos. In this sense, each generation acts as an incubator for this dynamic heritage, preserving and passing on cultural norms, ethics and beta as well as bringing fresh attitudes and perspectives. Though only a small percentage 'make the guidebook', the thousands of climbers who have spent time at the Rock, perhaps alone or working a project with friends, are the people who truly animate an otherwise static heritage. Outside of guidebooks and histories, the vivid sensations and emotions of countless climbers are embedded in real-time, providing the shared reference points around which a community of practice forms. In this manner, a rich and layered cultural geology has been laid down at Dumbarton Rock for the last 60 years. It is hoped this vibrant and distinct Scottish sporting heritage will one day be considered as our generation's contribution to Dumbarton Rock's remarkable history.

Ken Johnstone on 'Snowwhite' © Photo by Gary Latter

GEOLOGY

Dumbarton Rock is a volcanic plug that appeared in the Clyde valley after violent magma eruptions of the early Carboniferous period, or 'Trappean effusions' as they used to be called. The softer ash, tuffs and pumice were eroded by ice, wind, rivers and seas, leaving the hard candy core of the dome. Millions of years later, to Clyde valley quarries of the nineteenth century, the rock used to commonly be called 'whinstone' but has latterly more specifically been referred to as basalt. The British Geological Survey labels it more accurately as 'microporphyritic olivine-basalt', which might mean more to geologists – to climbers it is simply a solid, compact rock which is great to climb on. But looking carefully at the rock, there are more hues than suggested by the 'black Fontainebleau' nickname. The rock planes exhibit an olive or greenish tinge amongst its blacks, greys and ochres and it changes character with the seasons and diurnal shift of sunlight and shade, from distinctly moody and dark in winter to a dramatic flaming ochre in summer's sunsets.

Basalt is a rapidly cooled magma which is dense and compact. It is heavy and shears into blocky, fractured lines. Lifting a lump of sheared rock from around the boulders, a shard which was once part of a bigger whole, you can feel its heft and gravity and it seems to embody the weight of time and pressure within it. Around 340 million years ago Scotland was itself an embedded piece of the continent of Pangaea, sweating it out in equatorial regions, not having drifted to our current chilly latitude of 55 degrees north. Early tetrapod amphibians flopped around and huge plants such as *Equisetites* (giant horsetails) populated a rather steamy and frightening landscape as vents of lava poured from the troubled continental crust. Scotland was violent with earthquakes and exploding volcanoes and leaking faults. Magma was bleeding everywhere and throughout the geological periods from the Carboniferous to the Cretaceous lavas created our west coast archipelago, while quieter erosional times deposited sandstones, central valley limestones and coal seams which fuelled the industrial revolution.

As we drifted slowly north as part of a bigger tectonic plate for the next 340 million years, the continent split and the Atlantic began to flood into the valleys of the Clyde and Forth, laying down limestone in times of oceanic floods and sandstones in drier times. It must have been like a scene out of Tolkien's Mordor, with black smoke and fire and lightning in the clouds. The most vigorous igneous activity which birthed Dumbarton Rock occurred during the Visean Epoch (347–331 million

Night climbing © Ry McHenry

years ago). Somewhere in those millions of years, the crust spat out a great extrusion of magma which cooled to form the double-humped dome of Dumbarton Rock.

Due to its geological qualities, the Rock is protected in law as a Site of Special Scientific Interest (SSSI), described by Scottish Natural Heritage as 'a well-preserved and nationally important example of a volcanic plug of Lower Carboniferous age (around 340 million years ago) composed of Hawaiitic basalt', though it is hard to imagine the Hawaii connection while sheltering under the boulders from a typical winter squall.

Under the castle on the north shore, like scattered pieces of a 3D-jigsaw puzzle, lie massive volcanic boulders calved from the main crag. They can just about be re-imagined into place against the square-cut overhanging north-west face. Around 10,000 years ago, the boulders were shaken loose from the mother lode by violent earthquakes, caused as the vast ice caps of the last Ice Age rapidly melted and released their weight from the land below, causing it to rebound. The shattered dome left massively fractured faces and cracked walls, with a distinctly cubist look of flat planes, corners and clean lines.

This was the geological childhood of our central belt, our volcanic backdrop to a more recent human culture of heavy industries, fired metal and quarried rock. Dumbarton Rock will of course outlast its human culture and heritage, a testament to much bigger forces and the longer philosophy of stone.

Iain Pitcairn on 'Omerta' in 1993 © Gary Latter

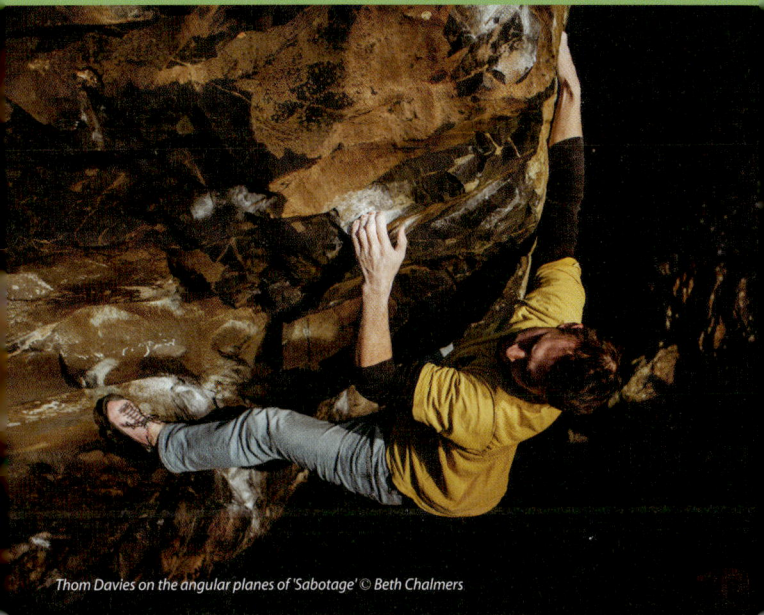

Thom Davies on the angular planes of 'Sabotage' © Beth Chalmers

Anna Hodgart enjoying Dumbarton's geology © Beth Chalmers

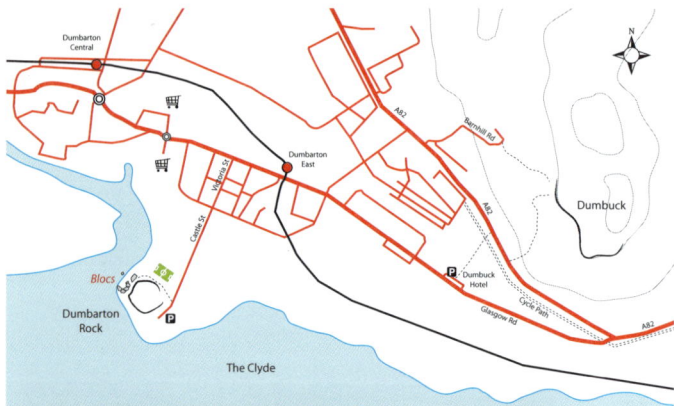

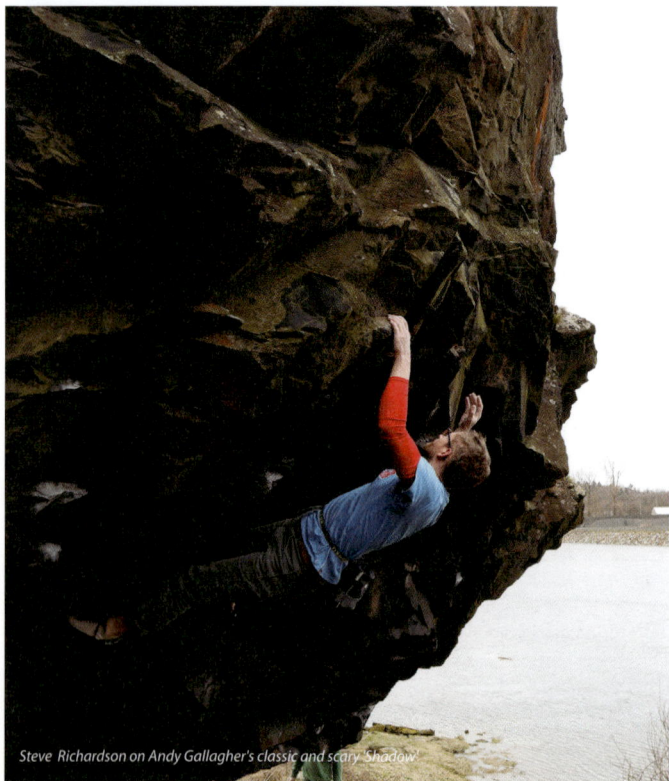

Steve Richardson on Andy Gallagher's classic and scary 'Shadow'

GETTING THERE

Grid Reference: NS 401 744

Post-code (for Sat Nav or Online Maps): G82 1JJ

Dumbarton is the last major town before Loch Lomond and is considered a gateway to the Highlands. The River Leven takes a short journey from Loch Lomond through the Vale of Leven to wind out into the Clyde estuary beside Dumbarton Castle. Dumbarton is 15 miles west of Glasgow city centre and is usually approached from the south and east via the M8 motorway to cross the Erskine Bridge onto the A82.

Dumbarton Rock's humped profile is easily visible on the north bank of the Clyde estuary. If approaching from the north or east, you will also be on the A82, so just follow signs into Dumbarton and then brown tourist signs to the castle. The castle is at the bottom of Victoria Street and its continuation Castle Street, not far from the railway station of Dumbarton East. Park beside the castle at one of the various parking spaces and take the old path along the base of the north side of the rock. The boulders and main faces appear suddenly beside the River Leven's estuary. As of 2020, Dumbarton Football Club's ground occupies the land in front of the approach to the crag, so it's worth checking when home games are played (usually a Saturday at 3 pm) when it can be impossible to park. They don't mind climbers walking across their car-park grounds as a shortcut to the crag. An upgrade to the old path on the north face is expected, linking eventually to a planned riverside walkway on the River Leven, thus threading access to Dumbarton town and the Castle and the coastal path beyond the Castle's eastern park.

By train: Regular trains run from Glasgow Queen St. low-level to Helensburgh Central and Balloch via Partick and Dumbarton. It takes about 25 minutes. Get off at Dumbarton East. Turn right at the bottom of the station, walk along 200m to turn left down Victoria Street to the castle.

By bike: The Forth and Clyde Canal bike path runs from Glasgow along the Clyde and through Kilpatrick and Bowling to Dumbarton. Just after Bowling and Milton, the cycleway passes under the dome of Dumbuck and into residential Dumbarton. About one hour from Glasgow.

Accommodation is sparse – there are a few B&Bs and budget hotels around Milton on the east side of Dumbarton on the A82. The nearest campsites can be found at the south end of Loch Lomond (such as Millarochy Bay), but if you have a camper van you should be able to find a spot to park near the castle for the night. Wild camping is not recommended at Dumby (it could be wild indeed).

SAFETY

Dumbarton Rock is, like any crag, susceptible to erosion and rock failure season by season, so care must be taken as part of the climbing experience. All climbers approaching the crag and boulders should assume their own levels of risk and accept responsibility for their ability and safety. It is wise to take accredited training on climbing safety techniques, and learn how best to protect your climb, whether traditional, sport or bouldering. These techniques are beyond the scope of this guidebook, so for safety techniques we would suggest visiting the *Mountaineering Scotland* website for courses (www.mountaineering.scot). For an ambulance or emergencies, call 999, or 101 for the Police.

THE CLIMBING

The traditional routes are found on the main 'Castle' wall or North West Face, on the Black Walls at the far west edge of the Rock, and on the approach path's North Wall, though this area is now extremely overgrown and would require significant gardening to bring it back to its best. The sport routes are found on the north-facing sidewall of the North West Face, as well on the right-hand side of the Black Walls area. Gear is often very good when the route follows a crack system, but the blanker faces tend to lend themselves to the sport routes or the harder, bolder

Neil Shepherd on 'Bad Atttitude' © Fraser Harle

extremes. Belays at the top of traditional routes occasionally have bolts but long slings are useful for finding solid belays further back. Descents are best by abseil from bolts at the top of *Chemin de Fer*, or from the top of the Black Walls. Please don't descend by accessing the Castle grounds and steps, unless in an emergency.

Dumbarton is a venue where the bouldering possibilities for link-ups and variations are endless. Aside from the 'original' problems from the 60s, 70s, and 80s, the more modern project-style problems add on sit starts or often lead to extensions, link-ups, eliminates and variations, so this guide attempts to be as comprehensive as possible without ignoring each generation's creativity in advancing the art of bouldering. Bouldering descents are usually on polished 'diffs' so take care to identify your descents before climbing.

A pertinent note to climbers is that the geology very much informs the style of climbing. The rock is a particularly fine-grained, compact and hard rock typical of 'Central Belt' basalt. Its typicality is that it shears into planes and crisp edges that unfortunately glass over quickly with traffic, making Dumby notorious for its tenuous friction and the need for perfect atmospheric conditions (a bit like Fontainebleau). Consequently, Dumby is at its best in cool conditions in a dry spell, as sustained wet weather makes it very green. That said, it can dry extremely quickly (20 minutes or so after heavy rain) and friction is often at its best after a rain shower and drying wind when locals talk of 'sticky damp'. A bitter wind makes it 'glassy' and seems to exacerbate the polished rock, particularly when combined with cold digits! Choose a still, sunny day in autumn, winter or spring for the best rewards. Shaded in the mornings, the sun creeps around and flares onto the rocks in the afternoon and evening. While climbing is possible all year round in the right conditions, summer can mean the rock sucks in radiation and becomes impossible to manage at the higher levels, so easy circuits or routes are recommended. The sport climbs on the main face come into better conditions in the summer months and rarely if ever see the sun. This is a trait shared with various faces of the boulders, so beware the greener aspects of the place, even in summer. Ground erosion and hold-wear is becoming a problem, with rubber coating precious footholds (which are often handholds) and making some problems harder. Fire damage is also an occasional issue as it shatters the rock, either creating new holds or leaving just nothing at all. When it all conspires against you and if the rain doesn't look like moving on, check out *The Glasgow Climbing Centre,* or *The Glasgow Climbing Academy*

Koon Morris on 'Bad Attitude' © Fraser Harle

(TCA), for a perma-dry climbing fix, or if the place is just too difficult, visit the outdoor bouldering park at Cuningar Loop beside the River Clyde (by Dalmarnock) in Glasgow's east end. All of these offer a good introduction to the art of bouldering.

GRADES

The traditional routes at Dumbarton are all graded with the mixed British notational system, e.g. E5 6b, the first grade representing the overall 'feel' and extremity of the route and the second grade reflecting the technical level of the climbing required. Dumbarton boulderers have traditionally used British technical (Brit) grades but modern boulderers favour the more divisional Fontainebleau (Font) grades. For the bouldering, British grades are mentioned historically in this guide where contextual, and many of the boulder problems are highball enough to be deemed mini-routes, and have traditionally been given extreme (E) grades for onsight attempts. For example, Andy Gallagher's first ascent of *Trick of the Vale* was deemed at once hard, bold and dangerous enough to warrant an initial E7 6c grade, but over the years this was whittled down, somewhat out of original context, through the security of mats, training methods, roped practice, video beta etc. Conscquently, we have largely avoided E-grades for the bouldering, as many easy problems are highball and can be just as dangerous with a simple slip, so we wouldn't wish to suggest some problems are 'dangerous' and some 'safe'. The word 'highball' applies to most Dumby problems, so it is not always repeated and problems should be considered as seen! It is always critical to use your judgment according to your ability, and worth understanding that the technicality of Dumbarton's climbing makes it an onsight challenge at all grades. French (F) sport grades are used for all the sport routes, e.g. F8a, and they have also been inserted where appropriate for the longer bouldering traverses as a useful cross-reference. All grades have been considered carefully and checked under consensus. Where a grade has been changed from previous publications it has been at the general agreement of the community.

THE ENVIRONMENT

Dumbarton can be a very pleasant green place in summer, but it comes with an urban environment's caveats and some anti-social baggage at times, though things are improving greatly with community development. A real problem at Dumbarton and one of its main detractions is that of litter. The river and tides wash a lot up, but some some people have no problem with leaving their litter behind without a thought, and

St Smith on 'Omerta' © Fraser Harle

Stuart 'Cobra' Lyall on the sport route 'Tarrier'

Will Atkinson on 'Sabotage' © Mike Scott

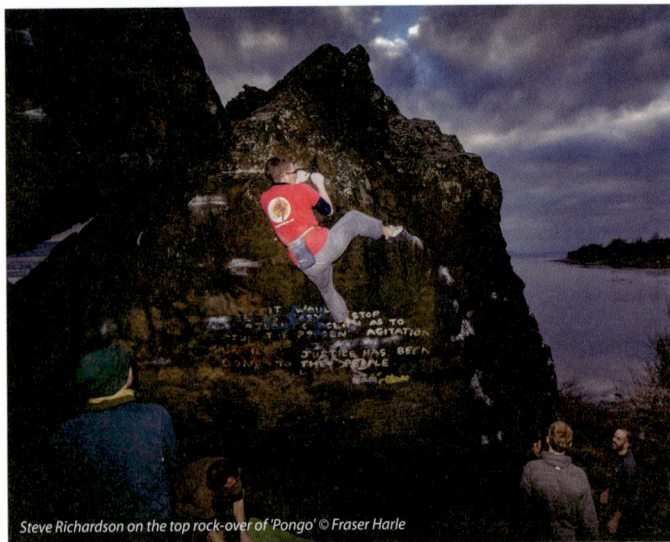

Steve Richardson on the top rock-over of 'Pongo' © Fraser Harle

the occasional barbecue or outdoor party can leave behind a mess. As climbers, we should take the lead and set a good example, tidying up when we can, as the litter quickly makes an eye-sore of the place and has given Dumby's attractiveness a bad reputation. To help keep on top of the litter, climbers often bring a bag (there are council bins at the car-park areas). Most years, a litter clean-up is organised by climbers, West Dunbartonshire Council and Historic Environment Scotland (HES) and this community respect for the place has significantly improved the overall appearance of this urban playground. Visual litter (graffiti) is impossible to prevent and hard to clean but does provide a telling social commentary: what was once political (the 'Bam Bam' era) has become more personal and colourful, but no doubt equally tribal.

If you are developing boulder problems or routes, please clean the rock carefully, don't use aggressive wire brushes, and please remove excess chalk and tick-marks. Choose your anchors for ropes carefully, as there are no bolts or anchors on top of the boulders so ropes have to be attached to ground anchors and draped over the boulders. This takes care and planning. Flattening landings with turf or gravel is fine but try not to alter the character of the starts. Erosion is a problem, so use mats where possible. Above all, just take care and look after each other!

WHO OWNS DUMBY?

Dumbarton Castle and its grounds, including the rock faces and most of the boulders, are owned and managed by Historic Environment Scotland (HES). This public body tolerates climbing on the faces and boulders despite the rock being designated a national monument. Relations with HES are good so please be respectful of the environment and do not access the routes by abseil through the castle grounds. Aside from this mutually agreed relationship, the laws of Scottish Access apply. Scotland's legislation for public access to the outdoors is egalitarian with the *Land Reform (Scotland) Act 2003* establishing a statutory framework of public access rights to most land and inland water. These rights are based on the principle of responsible access, with obligations both on the access users and on the managers of the land. Guidance on these responsibilities is set out in the Scottish Outdoor Access Code.

Every five years a geotechnical survey is done and the most recent established a reasonable rock stability and minimum rockfall risk. Climbers are advised by HES to climb at their own risk. The 'Dumbarton

Dave MacLeod on his 8b boulder problem 'Sanction'

Rock Liaison Group' (including climbers, HES, Scottish Natural Heritage and West Dunbartonshire Council) meets occasionally to discuss local development issues such as social use of the crag area, path development and general access issues. This group has a long-term vision for improving the environs of Dumbarton Rock for the benefit of all and the local community. There is usually an annual 'clean-up' as the litter grows over the summer, and this is advertised online every year, so if you are a Glasgow climber, even just for a while, consider coming along to these fun and social events.

Access from the castle grounds for top-roping crag routes is forbidden. Drilling bolts, whilst tolerated if done sensitively, contravenes the scheduled monument status of the Rock on which the castle stands ('A scheduled monument is a monument of national importance that Scottish Ministers have given legal protection under the Ancient Monuments and Archaeological Areas Act 1979' – HES). If access is required from the castle grounds to replace existing bolts, this should be discussed with HES, but most bolting can be accessed from the ground with existing in-situ bolts. Climbers must be aware of Historic Environment Scotland's stewardship of Dumbarton Rock and must look to their own insurances as any injuries are entirely the responsibility of those choosing to climb.

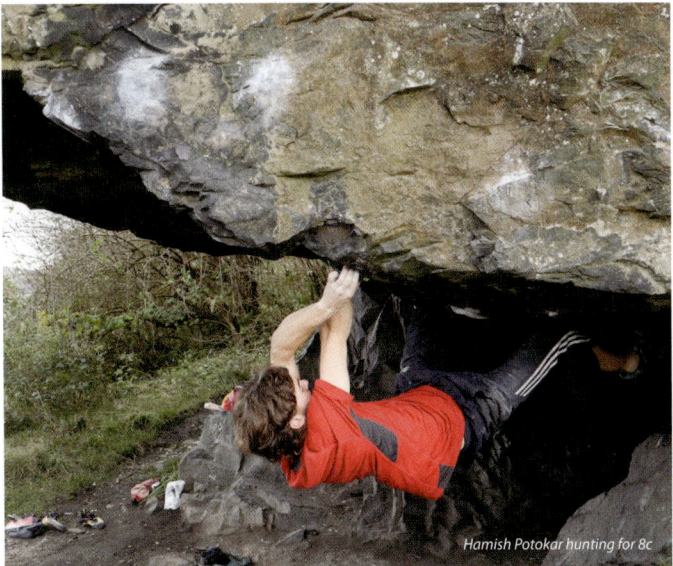

Hamish Potokar hunting for 8c

John Hutchinson on 'Sufferance' © Jonathan Bean

THE ROUTES

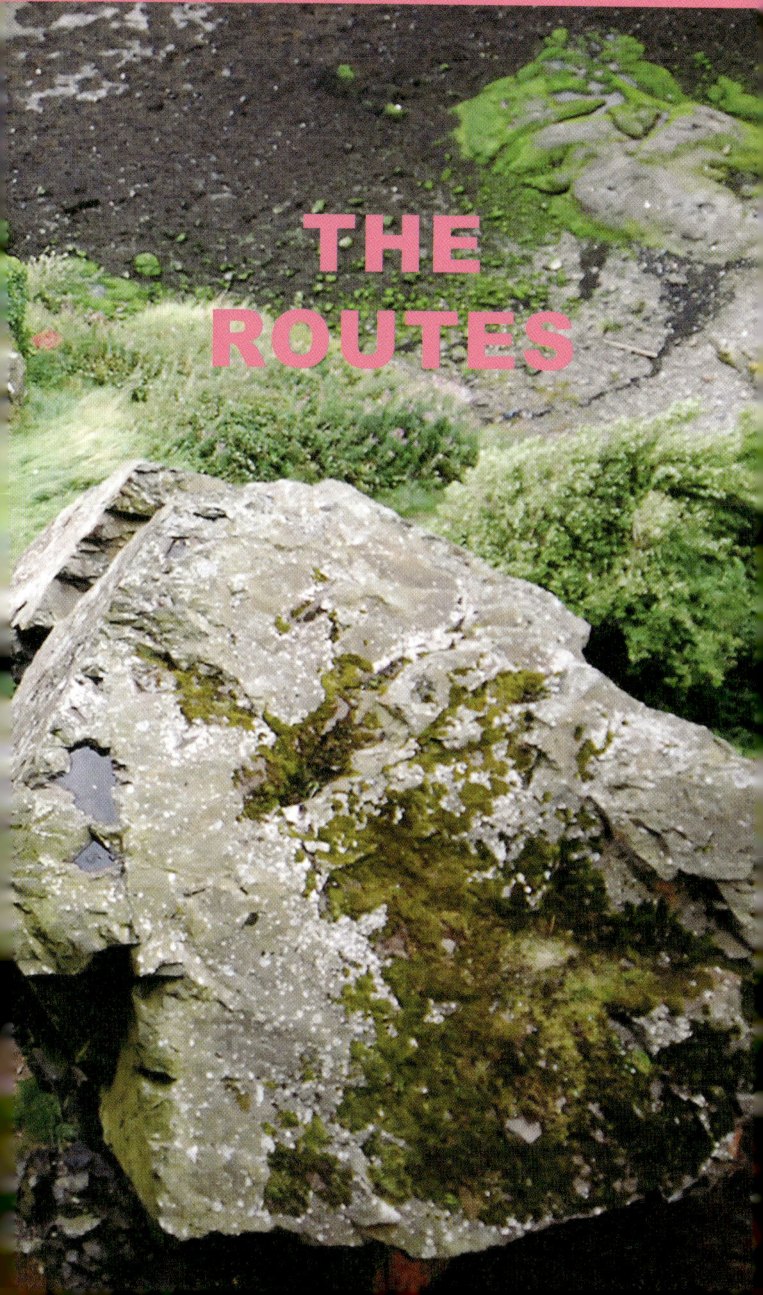

THE ROUTES

The impressive and intimidating main crag of the North West Face hosts the best of the traditional routes. Many trad routes on other aspects provide fine climbing too. Descent is by abseil from either fixed bolts or small trees. Do not descend by entering the castle grounds. Note, climbing is banned in the castle grounds, and on the east and south faces overlooking the castle entrance, despite routes having been done here in the past such as *L' Escargot* which climbed the east face and overhang above the car park (VS 4c, FA Ken Johnstone & George Christie, 1976).

THE NORTH WALL

The disappointing northern face of Dumbarton Rock overlooks the access path and used to be more popular in previous decades before it became neglected and overgrown. It suffers from its aspect and disintegrates with height into poor grassy finishes and dodgy belays, so consequently it needs some serious gardening and is rarely dry or clean enough to climb.

GULLY WALL SECTOR

This once-excellent shield of rock is now buried by ivy and vegetation, with the approach gully choked with trees and brambles, so the routes are all mentioned out of historical interest only. The wall runs up the steep slope at the end of the alleyway path.

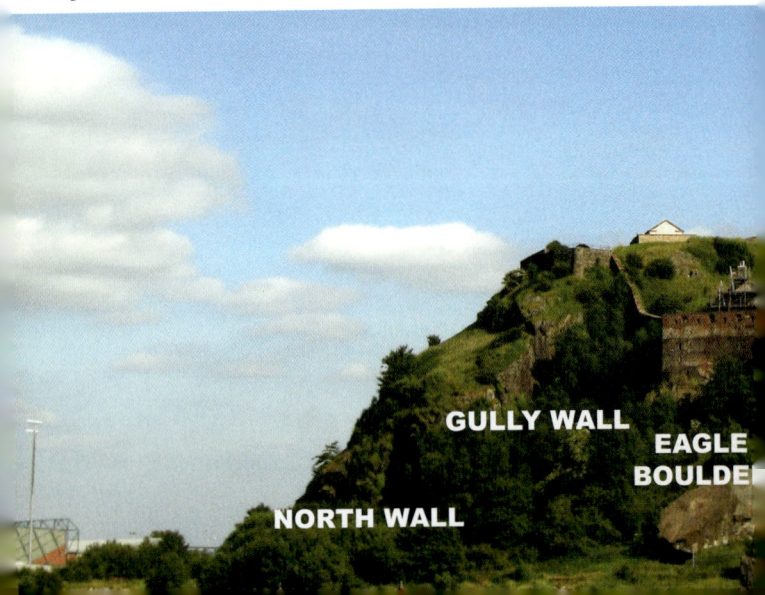

GULLY WALL

EAGLE BOULDER

NORTH WALL

NORTH WEST FACE

The intimidating steepness of the North West Face, with its two central cracks and fiery ochre glow in the evening sun, inspires a mixture of awe and terror. This is the home to the Rock's toughest trad and sports lines. Together with the adjoining shadowy right wall, with its collection of north-facing sport routes, the face comprises one side of a large open-book corner in the main dome of Dumbarton Rock. This giant missing section could be reconstructed from the boulders strewn below, a bit like a 3D rock jigsaw. Underneath the North West Face is a sector of mostly bolted 'slabs', which behave and feel more like a vertical wall when climbed and are the normal method of accessing the routes above. The climbing is everywhere technical.

BLACK WALLS & WEST SECTOR

These are the cornered black faces overlooking the River Leven estuary, between the last big boulders and the end of the grass platform. There are two prominent corners giving the best traditional lines of their grade at Dumbarton. The steeper walls to the right give some famously technical sports routes. The crags then diminish in height and continuity along the tidal section of the West Sector, underneath the castle walls, though there are a couple of worthy little crags with good rock. Unfortunately, ivy and vegetation seem to have taken hold on the top of these crags.

NORTH WEST FACE

BLACK WALLS

WEST SECTOR

NORTH WALL SECTOR

Ken Johnstone on the first ascent of 'Crackerjack', 1976 © Ken Johnstone

NORTH WALL SECTOR

❑ a. **Executive Wall** VS 4c

10m. An early route which Brian Shields described as 'a small wall with an arrow and the initials M.C.' Now covered in moss. FA M. Connolly, 1960s.

❑ b. **Alpha** HVS 5a

20m. Takes high twin cracks on the very left side of the face to grassy slopes and a belay far back. FA Gary Latter & Paul Laughlan, 1984.

❑ c. **Beta** E1 5b

20m. The next set of high twin cracks starting up slopey rock walls. FA Gary Latter, Paul Laughlan and Tam Meldrum, 1984.

❑ d. **Gamma** E1 5c

20m. Sloping rock ledges to the high steep crack left of the sloping ramps.

❑ e. **Uisge-Beatha** HVS 5a

25m. The left hand of the two higher sloping grooves, up broken ramps.

❑ f. **Rising Power** E2 5b

35m. A rightwards rising traverse from the ramps of *Uisge-Beatha*, taking a fault to the base of the *Antigrav* crack, taken briefly to a jug then rightwards again to finish up *Crackerjack*. FA Gary Latter & Paul Laughlan, 1984.

❑ g. **Bohert** HVS 5a

30m. Slopey ledges right of *Uisge-Beatha*, to enter the right-hand of the two diagonal ramps, finishing via a straight crack.

❑ h. **Antigrav** E3 6a

30m. A hard route on bold initial rock steps to the overlap bulge with a distinct thin crack above. Get good gear in the crack and launch up it. FA Ken Johnstone (2PA), 1977. FFA Willie Todd, 1979 (freed of two aid nuts).

❑ i. **Slàinte** E2 5c

30m. The right-hand of the thin cracks right of *Antigrav*. Up to the overlap and the crack to a small overlap and finish right. FA Ken Johnstone, 1970s.

❑ j. **Crackerjack** E1 5b

30m. Start just left of the midway recess. Climb the diagonal crack to ledges and continue up the excellent crack on the left wall above. FA Ken Johnstone & Dug McCallum, 1976.

NORTH WALL SECTOR

🔲 k. **Drizzle**   HVS 5a

30m. Climb the diagonal crack left of the big corner to a mantle right onto a big ledge. Climb the corner above finishing by its left arête. FA Ken Johnstone, April 1977. A bold E1 direct to the ledge was originally climbed.

🔲 l. **The Neilweg**   E1 5b

30m. Named after Dumbarton pioneer Neil Macniven. It climbs the big corner right of the crack of *Drizzle*. Gain a vegetated ledge higher up then finish up an exposed crack. FA Brian Shields & Michael Connolly, December 1964 (in two pitches).

🔲 m. **Boulevard**   VS 5a

30m. Mantle onto the rightwards-trending ramp of the recess and climb it rightwards to a grassy finish. FA Neil Macniven, 1963.

🔲 n. **Big Ears**   E1 5b

35m. Climbs a thin groove right of *Boulevard*. Mantle onto the ramp then up into a triangular niche, continue up grooves and finish by a higher crack. FA Gary Latter & Tom Prentice, 1981.

MONSOON GULLY SECTOR

Mostly vegetated now and rarely climbed.

🔲 a. **Hailstone Climb**   Severe 4a

30m. Originally given V. Diff., the walls and corners left of *Monsoon Gully* were originally climbed via grooves and ledges. Unstable, vegetated, with poor protection. FA Michael Connolly, 1964 (in a hailstorm).

🔲 b. **Left Edge Route**   VS 4c

30m. This originally climbed the left edge of *Monsoon Gully,* but it is no more after a 2002 rockfall. Not recommended due to unstable rock.

🔲 c. **Monsoon Gully**   Severe 4b

30m. The original description says it all: 'The large, wet, prominent gully. At the top, there is a delicate step left round a block. Finish by near-vertical grass.' FA Brian Shields & Michael Connolly, 1963.

🔲 d. **Supple as a Brick**   E4 5c

35m. Start up the gully then reach right on the steep wall to jugs, then launch boldly up grooves (RPs) to an overlap to easier territory, a ledge and

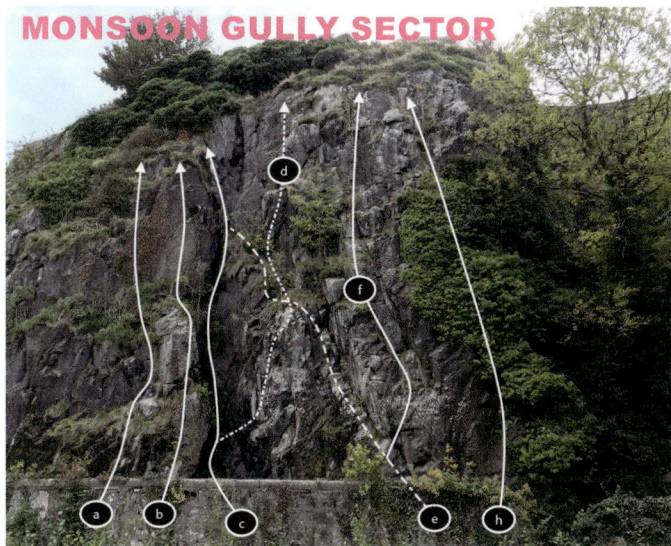

belay. Step 2m left and finish up grooves. FA Tom Prentice, Roger Everett & Simon Richardson, 1988.

☐ e. **Nameless Crack**   V Diff

25m. 'A pleasant route, which joins *Monsoon Gully* just below the crux.' (Brian Shields). Starts about 10 m right of the gully, taking the vegetated, left-trending crack line. FA Neil Macniven, 1964.

☐ f. **Alleyway**   VS 5a

25m. Start up *Nameless Crack* but take a rightwards shelf to grassy ledges and finish up blocks and grass. Originally climbed in two pitches. FA Neil Macniven, 1963.

☐ g. **Angel's Pavement**   VS 5a

90m. This is the oldest of the girdle traverses at Dumbarton. Originally climbed R-L from *Alleyway* to *Executive Wall*. The traverse is never more than 5m high, with the crux at the foot of *Boulevard*. FA (in 2 parts) N. Macniven. FA (complete) Brian Shields, 1964.

☐ h. **Sunset Groove**   VS 5a

30m. The vegetated groove at the right end of the wall before Gully Wall. Ivy-covered. FA Ian Fulton & Ian Nicolson, 1970s.

Brian Shields, belayed by Kenny Haggerty, on an early ascent of 'Ganglion Grooves'

GULLY WALL SECTOR

This once-excellent shield of rock is now largely buried by ivy and vegetation, though it may be possible to resurrect *Ganglion Grooves* and *Snowwhite*, the best routes on the wall. The wall runs up the steep slope at the end of the alleyway path just before the main area, with the castle walls at the top. The current approach is steep, slippy and barred by a lot of vegetation. Descent is best by abseil if this can be set up safely, or by traversing right to gain the gully and sliding back down this. The wall faces west and gets the afternoon and evening sun.

☐ a. **Ganglion Grooves**   VS 4c
20m. Climb a bulge to a flake and step right to the sloping foot-shelf. Surmount another bulge left and follow the main groove to a ledge near the top, traverse left and finish by a crack. FA K. Haggerty & Brian Shields, 5th August, 1964.

☐ b. **Ciamar a tha Sibh**   E2 5b
20m. Start as for *Ganglion Grooves* onto the sloping ramp, right to a short corner and the airy left arête. FA Andy Kelso, 1970s.

☐ c. **Snowwhite**   E2 5b
20m. The high crack right of *Ganglion Grooves* and *Ciamar a tha Sibh*. Start right of the corner and climb left to a short slab, then back right up steep rock to the crack, easing to the top. FA Andy Kelso (some aid), 1970s; FFA Willie Todd, 1970s.

☐ d. **Rag**   Severe 4a
15m. The grassy groove right of *Snowwhite*. FA Ian Nicolson, 1970s.

☐ e. **Tag**   HVS 5a
15m. Up right of the start of *Rag*. Follow the twin left-hand cracks and climb the wall above, then follow a groove on the left side of a block overhang. FA Ian Nicolson & R. McFarlane, 1970s.

☐ f. **Bobtail**   HVS 5a
12m. The furthest right route on the west wall. A short crack gains a groove, then make a crux move into the next groove and move left at the top. FA Steve Belk & J. Dalrymple, 1970s.

NORTH WEST FACE

Hugh Simons on 'The Big Zipper'. © Martin McKenna

NORTH WEST FACE

The main event, this wall needs no preamble to the clarity of its challenge.

❏ a. **Stonefall Wall**   E4 6a

10m. The white-streaked wall on the left face of the overhang. Descend the gully to the left under the castle wall, or abseil. FA Andy Gallagher, 1993.

❏ b. **Eliminator**   E6 6b

15m. The bold arête and headwall above the roof. Set-up a 'baby bouncer' of gear on *Stonefall Wall* and in *Route Three*. Climb the black arête to its end, place small wires, and take the headwall direct. FA Andy Gallagher, 1993.

❏ c. **Route Three**   HVS 5a

15m. Take the left side of the wall via a crack up to the big square roof, traverse right and finish up the chimney of *Stonefall Crack*. FA Brian Shields & K. Haggerty, 1964.

❏ d. **Stonefall Crack**   HVS 5a

20m. Originally graded VS. Enter the main crack directly below the higher chimney, then traverse diagonally left to the corner of the big square roof. Traverse right and finish up the old-school chimney. FA Neil Macniven, 1963. A later 'direct' ascent by Macniven and Shields climbed boldly up the crack at the same grade, but is much safer now with large modern gear.

❏ e **The Big Zipper**   E3 5b

30m. The overhanging cracked corner right of *Stonefall Crack*. Start up the direct version of *Stonefall*, then foot-traverse right (bold) on ledges to the crack, which is steep but well-protected. Take care the ropes don't drag! Bolt belay and abseil descent. FA (Aid) Brian Shields & A. Baillie, 23rd May, 1964 (in 4 ½ hours). The direct was climbed with two bolts by Murray Hamilton in 1977 before Gary Latter made a direct ascent freed of all bolts at E4 6c in 1983. The direct start is now retro-bolted as the start for *Omerta*.

❏ f. **Woops**   E4 6a

30m. The finger-crack right of *Stonefall Crack* to ledges under the corner, finish up *The Big Zipper*. FA Dave Cuthbertson & Ken Johnstone, 1980.

❏ g. **Rock of Ages**   E3 6a

20m. The rising right traverse from the base of *The Big Zipper* to the base of the *Requiem* crack and ledges. This was originally the pegged aid approach to *Requiem*. It is now a bold E3 requiring RPs. FA Gary Latter, 1983.

Stephen 'Fatboy' Horne on 'Chemin de Fer' © Martin McKenna

Niall McNair on 'Requiem' © Martin McKenna

❏ h. **Chemin de Fer**   E5 6a

30m. The striking and continual dog-leg crack on the overhanging face left of *Requiem*. Originally an airy aid route, it feels like a pumpy F7b sport route to onsight. The crack is good for placing gear, though it is increasingly strenuous and draining to do so. Start up ledges on the left and traverse right to the base of the crack where the intimidation begins. Place gear and launch up the crack via finger-locks and hand-jams. The higher part of the crack leads left with stamina-sapping moves to a cornered ledge. Many fall off at the final crack and begging mantelshelf. FA (Aid) Neil Macniven & Brian Shields, 1963. FFA Dave Cuthbertson & Ken Johnstone, 1980.

❏ i. **Achemine**   E9 6c

32m. The first of its grade in Scotland and a new-school line deliberately seeking out difficulty, with a big swing-fall potential. Take the *Chemin de Fer* crack to where it strikes left, place gear, then take the very bold and technical headwall above. First move through a small overlap, then go right on a handrail to a wee groove and hard moves upwards on small sidepulls. Move back left through a pinch to a crux traverse leftwards through a half-moon hold, and move up to jugs and rock over onto the ledges. About F8b climbing. FA Dave MacLeod, 2001 (11 long falls). The second ascent was by Barbara Zangerl in 2016.

❏ j. **Requiem**   E8 6b

35m. This stunning route takes the central crack of the overhanging main face. Originally an impressive A4 aid climb (done in midwinter), this is a classic modern free challenge, notably graded E7 for the original ascent in the 80s. Gain the base of the crack via the sport climb *Persistence of Vision* and strike up the crack, with layaways and jams, to a ledge and heel rest. From here, compose and strike rightwards up layaways in the shallow cracked corner to a sloping ledge (with final gear). Rock up left onto this to a crack and make a crux last move to the top ledges, from where it is commonly easy to fall with a long drop into space. FA (Aid) Brian Shields & Michael Connolly, December 1964. FFA Dave Cuthbertson, 1983. The first female ascent was by Caroline Ciavaldini in 2015.

❏ k. **Rhapsody**   E11 7a

35m. The hardest trad route on the planet when it was first climbed. The route takes the same initial crack line of *Requiem* but at the ledges it tackles the straighter challenge of the blank headwall to the apex of the face. Climb the initial crack of *Requiem*. At the 'resting ledges' after the crack section, go up on edges before trending left and then back right on edges

Niall McNair starting up the crack of 'Requiem'

Gary Latter on the second ascent of 'Cyclops', Photo by Ian Campbell

and sidepulls, then through a crossover move and further technical moves. The top section has a powerful double gaston sequence to a complex sidepulls sequence and a final lunge for the ledges just left of the apex. FA Dave MacLeod, 2006. Note, in 2008, Sonnie Trotter created a 'cop-out' finish at the American grade of 5.13c

❏ l. **Direquiem**   5.14a R (E10)
35m. A direct finish to *Requiem* or a straightened version of *Rhapsody*? Climbed by Sonnie Trotter in June 2008, it was a 'consequence' of his second ascent of *Rhapsody*. It goes direct and straighter than *Rhapsody* from the top of the *Requiem* crack to the top of the cliff. It was given the North American grade of 5.14a R, which translates as sport F8b+ climbing and the 'R' means that you can expect long but safe falls if you lob.

❏ m. **Cyclops**   E5 6b
35m. The big corner system on the right of the main face as it borders the sports wall is a hard E5 or softer E6. Pitch 1: 20m 5b Climb the bold and protectionless groove/corner on the right to a bolt belay on the grassy ledge. Pitch 2: 15m 6b Climb the overhanging corner past a peg to an easier higher section up a good crack. Abseil descent. FA (Aid) Brian Shields & K. Haggerty, 1974 (calling it *Resurrection*). FFA Dave Cuthbertson & Neil Cockburn, 1982.

❏ n. **Calm Before the Storm**   E6 6c
35m. The wall right of *Cyclops* is a bold outing. Climb the corner groove to the *Cyclops* grass ledge, place a Friend about 2m up the corner, step down. Traverse right across the wall diagonally on thinning holds to a crux sequence leading to jugs and easier but creaky climbing directly to the top. FA Dave MacLeod & Steve Richardson, 2003.

❏ o. **Requiem Direct Start**   E3 5b
15m. This mossy wall right of *Persistence of Vision* is rarely climbed and is a typical bold affair of its time. It would benefit from some deep cleaning. FA Ben Masterton & Andy Wren, 1983.

❏ p. **Dumb and Dumber**   E7 6c
20m. Thin climbing up the wall left of *Persistence of Vision*. Climb to a perched block, find gear out on the left groove, then launch up the 'slab' with very crimpy climbing at the top to reach *Rock of Ages*, finish up this. FA Dave MacLeod, 1999.

NORTH WEST FACE SPORT ROUTES

Paul Williamson on the tricky last clip of 'Persistence of Vision' © Ry McHenry

NORTH WEST FACE SPORT ROUTES

☐ a. **Payback Time!** F7b+

15m. Needs new bolts. Originally took a thin crack left of *Woops* with RPs, then the bolted headwall left of *The Big Zipper*. FA Andy Gallagher, 1996.

☐ b. **Omerta** F7c

30m. The arête right of *The Big Zipper* corner is a tremendously exposed sport route. Climb the desperate direct crack start to *The Big Zipper* to a resting ledge. From here launch up the right side of the arête to a ledge. FA Andy Gallagher, 1993.

☐ c. **Unfinished Symphony** F8b+

22m. The first part of a futuristic project, this takes the blank wall left of *Requiem* and currently finishes at the big undercut at the top of the black streak. Climb *Persistence of Vision* to its top, then crimp and sidepull moves lead to the ledge which is taken rightwards to a big move into *Requiem*. Exit this immediately (crux) to re-join the bolt line at the frustratingly slopey ramp. More hard moves on positive holds lead to the undercut. Lower off. FA Alan Cassidy, 2013.

☐ d. **Persistence of Vision** F7a+

15m. The superb bolted 'slab' line directly under *Requiem*. Climb grooves and steps to a technical sequence onto the edges of the main slabby wall, trending left at the fourth bolt, then back right into the hanging groove and the lower-off. FA Andy Gallagher, 1997.

☐ e. **Eurovision** F7a

15m. *Persistence of Vision* for four bolts, then trend right through the wee roof to bolts leading to a lower-off under *Requiem*. FA Alan Cassidy, 2018.

☐ f. **First Movement** F6b+

15m. From a ledge a few metres up and right, climb the bolt-line to the arête at the top, and a lower-off by the grassy ledge. FA Alan Cassidy, 2013.

☐ g. **Abstract Movement** F6b+

15m. Climb *First Movement* to its penultimate bolt, then hand-traverse a ramp up right to join *Abstract Art*. FA John Hutchinson, 2014.

☐ h. **Abstract Art** F6c

12m. A short but technically enjoyable route up the rightmost line of bolts on the slabs. Better than it looks. FA Dave MacLeod, 2004.

NORTH SPORT WALL

NORTH SPORT WALL

The sport routes on the north-facing black wall are squeezed into this blank protectionless sector between the traditional routes. Often referred to as the 'Sufferance Wall'.

☐ a. **Dum Dum Boys**   F8a+
23m. The left-hand line of bolts. Climb the corner to below the bolt line. A hard sequence gains the base of the rising ramp, which is taken to ledges. Continue up the easier top section to a lower-off. FA Andy Gallagher, 1995 (given F8a). Reclimbed after a broken hold, 2019, by Simon Smith.

☐ b. **Sufferance**   F8a
22m. The crimpy masterpiece of Dumby sport, up the left-central line of bolts on the wall. The crux is a hard fingery traverse rightwards at one-third height, shortly followed by a deep rock-over before the finishing ledges. Once described as 'overhanging slab climbing'. FA Andy Gallagher, 1993.

☐ c. **Suffix**   F8a
24m. Climb through the *Sufferance* crux to the jug then move right to finish up *Tarrier*. FA Ross Henighen, 2006.

☐ d. **Tarrier**   F8a
24m. The right line of bolts on the wall left of the arête and a niche. Layback the corner feature then jump for the ledge and finish up intermittent cracks. The lower-off is shared with *Sufferance*. FA Mark McGowan, 1993.

☐ e. **Endurance**   F8a
24m. *Tarrier* direct into *Sufferance* by pressing the long vertical crimps above the foot rail. FA Will Atkinson, 2010.

☐ f. **Persistence**   F8a
24m. As for *Endurance* into *Sufferance*, then, from the jug, head rightwards into the top of *Tarrier*. FA Ross Henighen, 2011.

☐ g. **Tolerance**   F8b
25m. A rising traverse. Start up *Tarrier*, break left up the wall to a handrail and reverse the *Sufferance* traverse section to climb leftwards into *Dum Dum Boys*, finishing up this. FA Dave Macleod, 2003.

BLACK WALLS TRAD

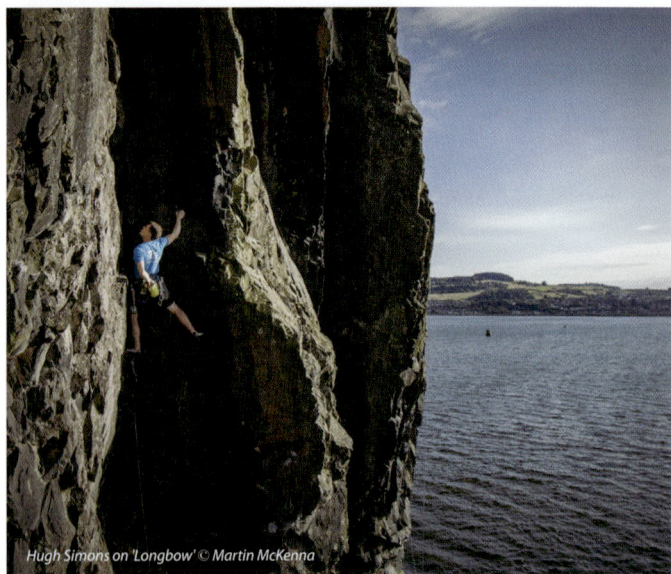

Hugh Simons on 'Longbow' © Martin McKenna

BLACK WALLS TRAD

Descent for all routes is via abseil from two bolts.

☐ a. **Fever Pitch**   E4 5c

25m. Take RPs! The flying arête on the left side of the wall. Climb to a horizontal break and gear, take the thin crux crack by the roof and trend right at the top. FA Nick Colton & Willie Todd, 1976.

☐ b. **Fatso**   E4 5c

30m. Takes *Fever Pitch* to the break, then a rising traverse up the wall to a spike. Go right then back left across a crux wall to finish as for *Fever Pitch*. FA Dave MacLeod, 1998.

☐ c. **Longbow**   E1 5b

30m. The first of the looming black corners is a delight all the way, with improving protection. Climb up the corner from the white arrow, step right at the top. Descent by abseil from bolts. FA (A3) Brian Shields & J. R. Houston 1964, done in February in two pitches with six wedges and seven pegs. FFA Steve Belk & J. Dalrymple, 1970s.

☐ d. **Eh Gringo**   E4 5c

30m. A serious and bold outing up the arête left of *Desperado*. Climb a hard groove 3m left of the corner then climb left on good holds to the slabs. Take the steep wall just right of the arête to a good undercut in an overlap, trending right through this, then back left to finish at the top of *Longbow*. FA Dave MacLeod & Richard McGhee, 2003.

☐ e. **Gaucho**   E2 5c

30m. Superseded by *Eh Gringo*, it climbed the cracked groove to the left of the corner to rejoin *Desperado*. FA Willie Todd & Nick Donnelly, 1976.

☐ f. **Desperado**   HVS 5a

30m. The hanging central corner is gained via 10m of *Windjammer* to a bold left traverse to the final corner. Descent by abseil. FA Brian Shields, 1970s.

☐ g. **Nil Desperandum**   E3 5c

30m. Start just right of *Longbow* and traverse right and up to join *Gaucho* just before it joins *Desperado*. FA Gary Latter, 1980.

☐ h. **Blackout**   E6 6a

30m. The ominous hanging arête left of *Windjammer* is serious and has

Peter Phillips on Windjammer

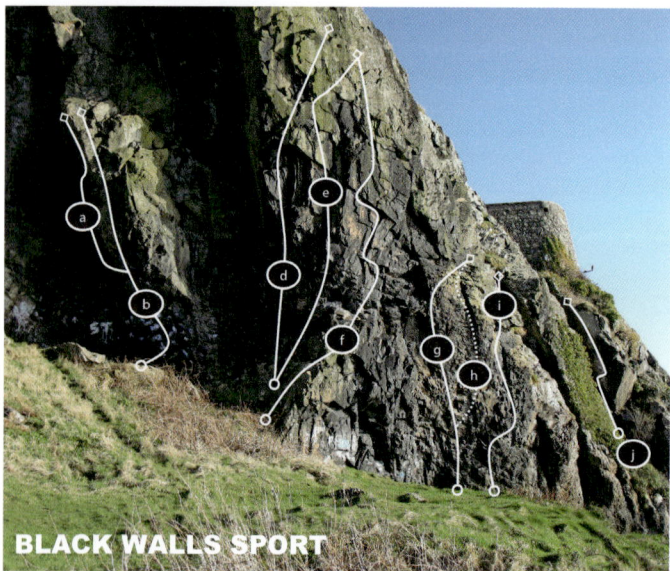

BLACK WALLS SPORT

dubious gear in the higher section. Climb *Windjammer* to the base of the arête, continue up the crack for 3m then move out left to the arête on undercuts. The technical arête has its crux at the top. FA Dave MacLeod & Steve Richardson, 2003.

❑ i. **Windjammer**   HVS 5a
30m. The right-hand corner gives excellent bridging and crack climbing to a thrilling layback finish up the large flake at the top, turned on its right. Descent by abseil. FA Brian Shields & J. R. Houston, 1964.

❑ j. **Rough Sea**   E2 5b
30m. A bold route, originally given HVS! Climb *Windjammer* to a junction and take the flakes leading right to the bold arête. Climb the wall on the right to the top. FA Ken Johnston & Martin 'Harpic' Hind, 1977. Named after an oil rig which was docked in the Leven at the time.

❑ k. **Friends in High Places**   E4 6a
35m. Takes the groove right of the bottom bouldering wall in an overhanging niche, then right into a hard section through overlaps to a tricky exit right. Move right again and finish up grooves. FA Dave MacLeod, 1998.

❑ l. **Knees and Toes, Knees and Toes** E4 5c
40m. Climbs hard right over the drop-off to a pod, up to the crack of *Natural Born Drillers*. Place a large friend here and traverse right to the blunt arête until an escape left leads to slabbier rock and a finishing corner and grooves. FA Dave MacLeod & Bob Ewen, 1998.

BLACK WALLS SPORT

The bolted lines on the blanker walls are technical. Lower offs.

❑ a. **Negative Creep**   F8b
10m. Start up *Appliance of Violence* but break left after the fourth bolt onto the overhanging wall left of the hanging arête. Take sidepulls to a desperate crux Egyptian at the top leading back right to the ledges at the lower off. FA Dave MacLeod, 2004.

❑ b. **Appliance of Violence**   F7b+
10m. The hanging arête route is short but great fun and very popular. Climb up the chalky crack at the bottom to a technical sequence through sloping ledges to the arête, layback up this to the lower-off. FA Benny McLaughlan, 1993.

Neil Shepherd on 'Bad Attitude' © Fraser Harle

❐ c. **Gratuitous Violence**   F8a

15m. Traversing into the base of *Appliance of Violence* along the *Shattered Low Traverse* is a contrived but fun 8a, considered a worthwhile training route for the grade. FA Pete Roy, 2010.

❐ d. **Bad Attitude**   F7b

18m. The groove system just right of *Windjammer* is technical, with glue-in bolts. FA Andy Gallagher, 1993.

❐ e. **Half Breed**   F7b

18m. The next groove system to the right eventually trends right above the roof section to lower off *Unforgiven*. FA Cameron Phair, 1993.

❐ f. **Unforgiven**   F7b

18m. The exposed wall to the right starts up a rising right traverse from the *Windjammer* corner. A committing step left on a poor foot-sloper leads to a technical overlap section and a more straightforward top section. Some people use a high gaston at the crux. FA Andy Gallagher, 1993.

❐ g. **Benny's Route Left**   F7b

10m. The lower wall before the drop-off has a steep scoop section on shattered rock. Trend left at the third bolt to the blunt arête and then climb back right to the lower off. FA G. Sutcliffe, 1994.

❐ h. **Benny's Route**   F7c

10m. The original 'right-hand' route makes hard moves right from the third bolt then takes the fault directly to the lower off. FA John Dunne, 1993.

❐ i. **Natural Born Drillers**   F7a

12m. The traverse line of bolts out right over the drop-off is a popular route. Climb out to the hanging crack and surmount the bulge with difficulty onto slabs to the lower off. FA Cameron Phair, 1996.

❐ j. **Casanostra**   F6c+

10m. Now fully re-equipped with resin bolts and lower off, this burly sport route is started halfway up the West Face Gully on the steep right wall. Access to the gully is only possible at low tide. A bouldery step-on sequence leads to an easier finish up the overhanging groove on good holds. FA Andy Gallagher, 1997.

SOUTHWEST GULLY SECTOR

RED SLAB SECTOR

SOUTH WEST GULLY

❑ a. **Dumbarton Chimney**   VS 4c

30m. The chimney left of the gully is vegetated and not recommended.

❑ b. **Silly Thing**   HVS 4b/5b

40m. Originally two pitches up the large corner, with a block belay under the top pitch which is a steep crack. Ivy-covered. FA Gary Latter & Mick McGahan, 1979.

❑ c. **Easter Rib**   Severe 4a

20m. The lovely rib left of a roofed corner. FA Andy Gallagher, 1999.

❑ d. **Frendo**   VS 4c

30m. From the gully, a narrow ramp left to slabs. FA Brian Shields, 1963.

❑ e. **Grey Slab**   VS 5a

25m. At the top of the gully, take the steep slab to a common finish with Frendo. FA Brian Shields & Michael Connolly, 1964.

❑ f. **West Face Gully**   Severe 4a

20m. The gully originally climbed into the castle. FA Brian Shields, 1965.

RED SLAB SECTOR

❑ a. **Plunge**   Difficult

30m. The vague ridge right of the old mooring ring. Traverse right at the top under the castle wall. Rig an abseil descent. FA L. Mitchell, 1960s.

❑ b. **Route 66**   Severe 4a

40m. Climb *Plunge* but go left to bridge a gap at the gully to a corner. FA Brian Shields, Kenny Haggarty & A. Baillie, 1964.

❑ c. **Red Slab**   Hard Severe 4b

10m. The cracked red slab right of *Plunge*. Belay or abseil from the tree.

❑ d. **Old Socks**   Hard Severe 4c

10m. The cracked overhang right of *Red Slab*. FA Brian Shields, 1960s.

❑ e. **Poison Ivy**   VS 5a

10m. 7m right of *Old Socks*, climb the delicate red slab. Belay or abseil from the tree. Or scramble down left if soloing. FA Brian Shields, 1964.

PINKY CRAG

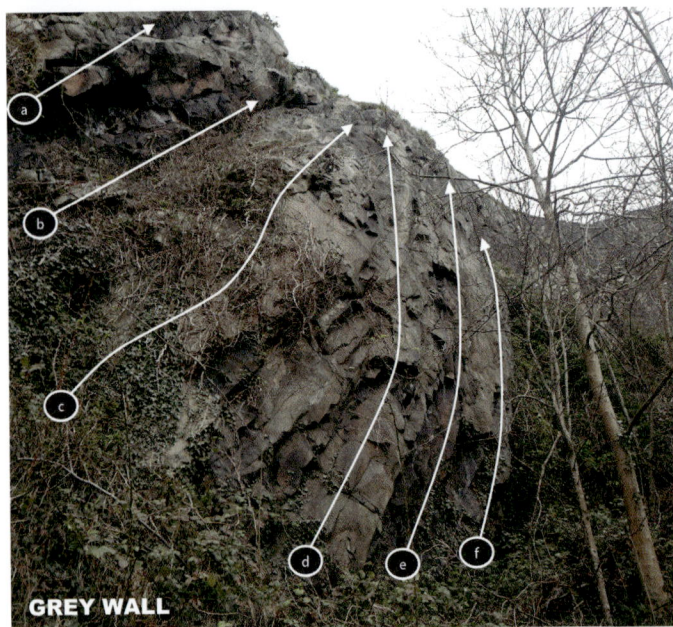

GREY WALL

PINKY CRAG

This little crag under the castle wall has a blackish groove and overhang on its right side. Rig an abseil at the top.

❑ a. P**inky**   VS 4b
12m. This takes the left-hand rib/groove.

❑ b. **Perky**   Hard Severe 4b
12m. This route takes the central overhang's groove on the left.

❑ c. **Still Going**   HVS 5a
12m. Climbs the right-hand groove and the overhang, taken on the right.

GREY WALL

The crag under the castle walls amongst trees right of Pinky Crag. It may need significant gardening before any ascents. The rock is compact but beware loose blocks. Protection is scarce and the routes are bold. The last three routes are effectively solos.

❑ a. **Banana Rib**   V Diff
15m. The slanting rib on the left of the dark groove. FA Ian Fulton, 1970s.

❑ b. **Banana Groove**   VS 4c
15m. The diagonal black groove. FA Ian Nicolson & R. McFarlane, 1970s.

❑ c. **Banana Slide**   E1 5a
15m. Climb the wall to the right of the groove to the arête and trend right at the top. FA Ian Nicolson & R. McFarlane, 1970s.

❑ d. **Grey Wall**   E4 5c
15m. Climbs the grey rock on the right, past a hanging flake at half-height, with the crux at the top. A serious solo with no gear. FA Gary Latter & Andy Wren, 1983.

❑ e. **Datura**   E3 5c
12m. 3m uphill from *Grey Wall*, at a downwards flake. Climb the wall direct over two ledges. FA R.Kerr, solo, 1980.

❑ f. **Samora**   E3 5c
12m. Start right of *Datura* and take a line rising to the ledge at its right end, finish direct. FA Gary Latter, solo, 1984.

John Hutchinson high on 'Physical Graffiti'. Photo: Jonathan Bean

THE
BOULDERING

DUMBY SECTORS

SECTOR 27
SEA WALLS

Castle Grounds

BLACK WALLS

Requiem E8

SPORT WALLS

SECTOR 26
BLACK WALL

NORTH WEST FACE

SECTOR 25 EVERDRY WALL

Chemin de Fer E5

Descent

SECTOR 18
GOOD NICKS

B.N.I.

SECTOR 10
VALHALLA

SECTOR 16
SUCKER'S SLAB

Descent

SECTOR 19
BNI SLABS

SECTOR 11
BEAST SLABS

SUCKER'S

Descent

SECTOR 17
WALKTHROUGH CAVE

HOME
RULE

SECTOR 12
MUGSY ROOF

SECTOR 15
SHIELD WALL

Descent

SECTOR 14
ROUTE ROYALE

SECTOR 13 HOME RULE

PONGO

SECTOR 20
PONGO FACE

SECTOR 22
CONSOLIDATED

TIDAL

SECTOR 9
WARM-UP WALL

SECTOR 23
TRIPLETS

SECTOR 1
EAGLE SLABS

SECTOR 21
PONGO SLABS

Descent

SECTOR 2
PULLOVER

SECTOR 8
BLUE MEANIE

SECTOR 3
ZIG ZAG

EAGLE
BOULDER

PLINTH

TIDAL

SECTOR 7
EAGLE FACE

SECTOR 4
SHADOW WALL

Descent

SEA
BOULDER

SECTOR 5
GORILLA CAVE

SECTOR 6
GORILLA PROW

SECTOR 24
SEA BOULDER

TIDAL

Parking via path

Parking via shore

N

0m   5m   10m

EAGLE BOULDER

The giant prow boulder is first seen on the approach, under the main face. The boulder is named after a now-vanished eagle painted on the slabs in the 1960s (superseded by a Lion Rampant). Descent for all problems is via the ledges facing the main face, polished by a long history of many boots and shoes. It has four distinct facets with varying steepness from slabs to leaning walls to a flying northern roof and the famous 'Gorilla' prow.

HOME RULE

The large, cubist bloc above the warm-up wall, with a high north face. This used to host 'Home Rule' graffiti in the 1970s. The problems are described in an anti-clockwise direction from the back chasm slabs round to a caved 'Mugsy' sector, the 'Home Rule' wall and the 'Route Royale' walls.

WARM-UP WALL

This is the lower boulder wall under Home Rule, with a flat grassy landing, with walk-off descents. This is officially the least scary spot at Dumby and the best place to warm up.

SUCKER'S BOULDER

This is the boulder jammed in between the higher boulders of Home Rule boulder and the tall B.N.I. boulder. It is characterized by a leaning seaward face and a hanging ramp above. It sports the classic hard problem of *The Shield* but also has easier perched slabs at the back right.

B.N.I. BOULDER

This is the tall boulder with various hanging walls above a walk-through cave sector adjoining the lower Pongo boulder. Originally named due to its reputation as being 'Bloody Nigh Impossible', the sectors comprise the walkthrough cave, the hanging slabs of B.N.I., and the perched slabs above the Pongo descent.

PONGO BOULDER

This is the lower boulder with the overhanging crack on the north-east face ('Pongo'). The westerly faces are more slabby in nature, steepening towards the walkthrough cave sector at the end of the 'Consolidated' traverse.

SEA BOULDER

The partly tidal bloc on the shore has four facets with arête problems.

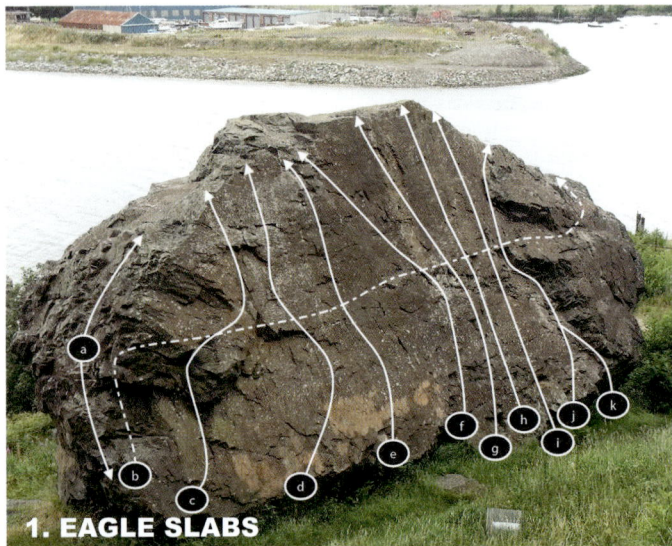

1. EAGLE SLABS

Stewart Brown in period costume on the slabs

SECTOR 1: EAGLE SLABS

The tall slabs are shady and can be a bit dirty after a long winter, so take care.

❑ a. **Descent Route**   1

The polished staircase bounding the left arête is the easiest descent.

❑ b. **Girdle Traverse**   3+

Start up *Descent Route*, then traverse the slabs at mid-height to finish right past *Zig Zag* and continue to gain the ridge on the far right, then up left to the top. Taking a lower line makes it easier, but is also good.

❑ c. **Rankin's Bajin**   3

The slab 1m right of *Descent Route*, on right-trending holds to a small overlap near the top. FA Brian Shields & Michael Connolly, 1960s.

❑ d. **Soixante Neuf**   3+

3m right of *Descent Route*. Trend up right to a sloping foot ledge, then take the headwall through a letterbox feature to the top. FA Neil Macniven, 1960s.

❑ e. **Pas Mal**   3+

Just left of the plinth. Climb up the slab to join the top of the ramp. FA Michael Connolly & Brian Shields, 1960s.

❑ f. **Number One Route**   2

The easy R-L ramp via large holds. Start 1m right of the midway rock plinth.

❑ g. **Left Direct**   3+

Right of the plinth to the ramp ledge, then direct up the wall via left-facing flakes. FA Brian Shields & Michael Connolly, 1960s.

❑ h. **Centre Direct**   4

The hardest line on the slabs takes the slab direct at its blankest and highest section. Start just left of where the slab begins to overhang. FA Neil Macniven, early 1960s.

❑ i. **Right Direct**   3+

Take the slab just to the right again, easy at first, but leading to a harder direct finish to the left of the flake of *No. 2 Route*. FA Brian Shields & Michael Connolly, 1960s.

❑ j. **Number 2 Route**   3

Start as for *Right Direct* but move more easily rightwards to the top up the corners and high flake.

❑ k. **Number 2 Direct**   4+

Start right of the jutting nose at a large jug on the lip of the overhang, then mantle into the groove above. Trickier than you might think.

2: PULLOVER SECTOR

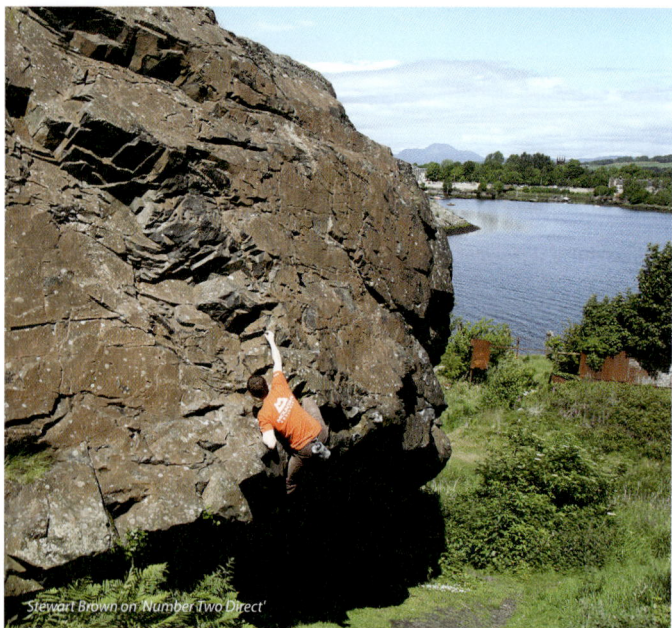

Stewart Brown on 'Number Two Direct'

SECTOR 2: PULLOVER

The long overhang undercutting the slabs on the right gives steep climbing.

❑ a. **Double Bogey** 6b

Sit start in the groove with a right hand in a shallow shot-hole, left hand on a low, undercut pinch. Pull on and slap the right hand to a sloper on the lip, gain a higher hold and mantle into the groove. FA John Watson, 2012.

❑ a1. **Triple Bogey** 6c

As for *Double Bogey*, but traverse hard left along the low lip to a squeezed groove mantle onto the slab via a crimp and lunge to a grassy pod. FA John Watson, 2012.

❑ a2. **John's Dyno** 6c

Sit start in the groove, right hand in the shallow shot hole, left hand on a thin crimp under the lip. Pounce to a jug and mantle into the groove. FA John Watson, 2012.

❑ b. **Kev's Problem** 7a

Crouch start at two poor undercuts, pulling on with a right foot on a low ledge, then gain the inset hold with the left hand. Twist up to a smooth right-hand hold and slap through slopers to the jugs of *Pullover*. A true sit is 7a+. FA Kevin Grant, 1996.

❑ b1. **Runs on Potato Power** 7a

Crouch start as for *Kev's Problem* but go to the inset with the right hand. Gain the thin vertical pinch/crimp for the left and slap for the jugs. FA Dave MacLeod, 1998.

❑ b2. **Kev's Chop Problem** 7a+

Sit start on *Kev's* undercuts, climb out right to the sloper/pinch on *Bust My Chops* and finish onto slab. FA Thom Davies, 2020.

❑ c. **Pullover** 5

From the big jug on the lip 4m right along the roof, pop up and left to a flatty and pull onto the slab. Harder for the short. FA Neil Macniven, 1960s.

❑ c1. **Pullover Traverse** 5+

Sit start at the furthest left side of the roof, left of a wee nose. Traverse right along the lip to the starting jugs of *Pullover* and do so.

❑ d. **The Beastie** 6a

A stand-up to the top of *Bust My Chops*. Stand under the big sloper at the wee nick on *Kev's Problem*, jump for the flat hold above the sloper and rock right onto the slab.

❑ e. **Old Faithful** 5

The line just left of *Zig Zag*, climbed direct. From finger-jugs on the lip climb up onto the slab via finger layaways in a vague crack, rock onto the slab with interest and finish direct up the slab.

John Watson on 'Zig Zag'

3: ZIG ZAG SECTOR

SECTOR 3: ZIG ZAG

This sector includes mostly modern sit starts and link-ups on the leaning wall from *Pullover* rightwards to *Bampot Arête*. The main reference problem is *Zig Zag*.

❑ a. **Bust My Chops**   7a

Sit start at the low slopey shelf. Gain the twin crimps above and then slap the left hand up to a right-facing corner sloper (some use an intermediate and very poor lip crimp). Twist up to good holds above and rock onto the slab directly. Originally 7b until a crimp inset broke and improved. FA Dave MacLeod, 1998.

❑ a1. **Bust My Chops (Left)**   7a

Sit start and gain the left-hand slot and right-hand crimp. Heel hook out right and cross over the right hand to the sloper-pinch. Snap left to finish up *Pullover*.

❑ a2. **Bust My Chops (Right)**   7a

From the twin crimps gain the lip and go right to a knobbly hold, pull over direct on edges. FA Dave MacLeod, 2001. A slightly easier version takes the big flat hold on the right and finishes via *Zig Zag*.

❑ a3. **Bust Jeremy's Chops**   7a

As for *Bust My Chops* but from crimps stretch far right to finish up *Jeremy's Problem*.

❑ a4. **The Ramp**   6c+

Sit start at *Bust My Chops* at the ramp's crimped sloper. Traverse rightwards past the big flattie and keep going on the lip slopers to rock right round *Bampot Arête* and onto the slab on *Tam's Route*. A shortcut finish up the *Zig Zag* jugs makes it 6b.

❑ b. **Zig Zag**   4

Classic stopper. Pull over the roof onto the hanging slab via a protruding chalky jug, then step right then nervously back left through overlaps. Finish direct or up the easier groove leftwards. FA Neil Macniven, 1960s.

❑ b1. **Zig Zag Sit Start**   6b+

Sit start with sidepulls and gain the lip via a sidepull/pinch and finish as for *Zig Zag*.

❑ b2. **Zig Zag Super Low**   6c+

Start almost lying down in the pit by the foot-ledge, sharp juggy flake for the right and small crimp for the left. Move up to another poor hold for the left hand, maybe made a bit easier by sitting on the right heel.

❑ b3. **Double Slopers**   6a+

Crouch start from the undercling. Stab feet on and slap straight up to match the lip slopers, then jump for the *Zig Zag* jug directly and finish up this.

Colin Lambton on 'Treasure Hunt'

John Hutchinson on 'Bampot Arête' © Photo Sam Scriven

❐ b4. **Jeremy's Problem** 6c+
Starting as for *Double Slopers*, ignore jugs and aim up left for a sloping pinch, then lunge for the highest flatty above, pull up and onto the slab.

❐ b5. **Treasure** 7b
Zig Zag Sit Start to the ramp, traverse left to finish up *Bust My Chops (original)*.

❐ b6. **Treasure Hunt** 7b
Zig Zag Sit Start to the ramp, traverse left into *Bust My Chops (Left)*.

❐ b7. **Fool's Gold** 7a+
Zig Zag Sit Start to the ramp, traverse left and finish up *Bust My Chops (Right)*.

❐ c. **Bampot Arête** 6b+
Sit start the black arête from a very low left-hand crimp and right hand just below a sloping ledge. Cross through to the slopey ledge, then gain a right-hand flatty. Don't get lured further right (*Tam's Route*) but throw directly up left to a crimp on the lip left of the arête. Mantle onto the slab and finish left via *Zig Zag*.

❐ c1. **Bampot Traverse** 6c+
Eliminate. *Bampot Arête* but traverse the lip left to the double slopers, then make a direct crux move all the way to the jug on *Zig Zag* (ignoring jugs left of slopers).

❐ c2. **Total Bampot** 7a
Up *Bampot Arête* then traverse the lip left to the double slopers, then take the higher line of good holds left above *Bust My Chops* to finish onto the hanging slab above.

❐ c3. **The Chop** 6c+
Sit start at a right-hand pinch on the arête, left hand on a thin sidepull, slap up to a sidepull pinch on the shield, gain the lip and mantle the slab. FA John Watson, 2012.

❐ c4. **Total Bamchop** 7a+
Sit start up *The Chop*, traverse left through the *Double Slopers* and finish along *Total Bampot*.

❐ c5. **Treasure Trail** 7b+
Bampot Arête, then traverse left through *Double Slopers* and low into the slot and crimp of *Bust My Chops*, finish low left and up *Pullover*.

❐ c6. **Fouk Ye** 7b
A hard eliminate of *Bampot Arête*. Sit start and twist into a wide, open pinch on the arête and flick leftwards to sidepulls to finish left into *Zig Zag*. FA Andy Earl, 2001.

❐ c7. **Fouk Yer Chops Kev** 7c
Treasure Trail but do the eliminate start to *Fouk Ye*. FA Stewart Brown, 2010.

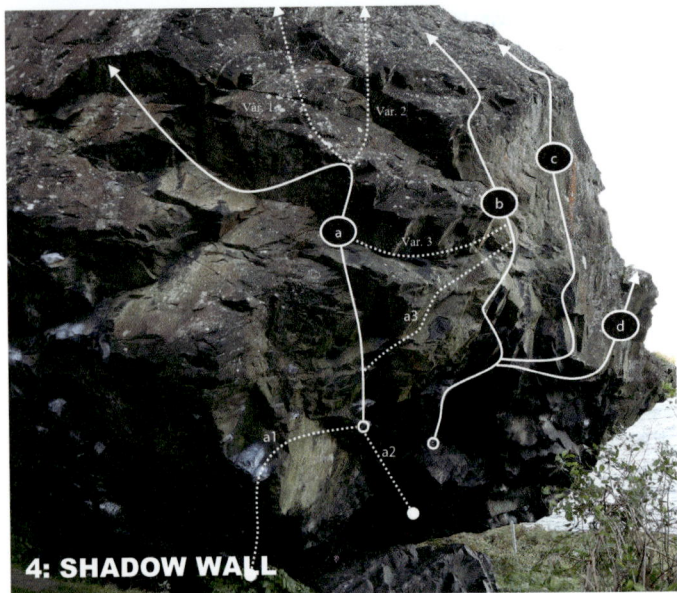

4: SHADOW WALL

Steve Richardson on 'Tam's Route'

SECTOR 4: SHADOW WALL

The terrifying shadowed north roof and wall over a difficult landing. Rarely climbed, and mostly after abseil cleaning and inspection. Mats and spotters essential.

☐ a. **Tam's Route** 5+

A legendary old school classic, taking the groove and walls right of *Bampot Arête*. Stand on the plinth and crank up the leaning groove on flatties. At the top of this, a slab sidepull and a high lip hold allows a rock-over left onto the short slab. FA Tam 'The Bam' McAuley, 1970s. The original finish traversed left into *Zig Zag* but several alternative highball finishes have been done: over the roof direct; over the roof but go slightly right using a thin pinch/flake for the left hand. There is also a harder 6a foot traverse finish rightwards into the top section of *Shadow* (FA Andy Gallagher).

☐ a1. **Tam's Route Sit Start** 6a+

Sit start *Bampot Arête* but cross right into the flatties of *Tam's Route* and finish up this.

☐ a2. **Tam's Route Sit Right** 7a

Squeeze into the sit start ledge left of *Shadow*. Pull on using a right-hand sidepull and slap up to jugs to join the original problem. Considerable body tension required. FA Dave Macleod, 2005.

☐ a3. **Tam's Shadow** 6c+

Sit start as for *Bampot Arête* then cross the jugs of *Tam's Route* into the left ramp on *Shadow* and finish up this. Harder if the direct SS to *Tam's Route* is done.

☐ b. **Shadow** 7a

A classic hard highball, this takes the overhanging black groove right of *Tam's Route*. Start from good edges at the back of the groove, crank backwards and left to a sloping hold and use a polished high step to go right to a sharp crimp. Hard pinches above lead to better holds and a reach to the flat holds at the base of the top slab. From here, balance onto the slab to finish up the ridge of the boulder. FA Andy Gallagher, 1992.

☐ c. **Trick of the Vale** 7a+

Start as for *Shadow,* but match the sharp right-hand crimps and crank up the right side of the groove. Step right onto a rising slab ledge for a tentative rest. Compose and climb direct up the wall to the apex to gain a tricky sequence onto the finishing slab. Committing and hard. FA Andy Gallagher, 1992.

☐ d. **Story of the Hurricane** 7a

Climb as for *Trick of the Vale* but hand traverse right along the big ramp with airy moves to an exciting top-out. From the end of the ramp, take juggier holds onto the front slab of the boulder. FA Steve Richardson, 2011.

5: GORILLA CAVE

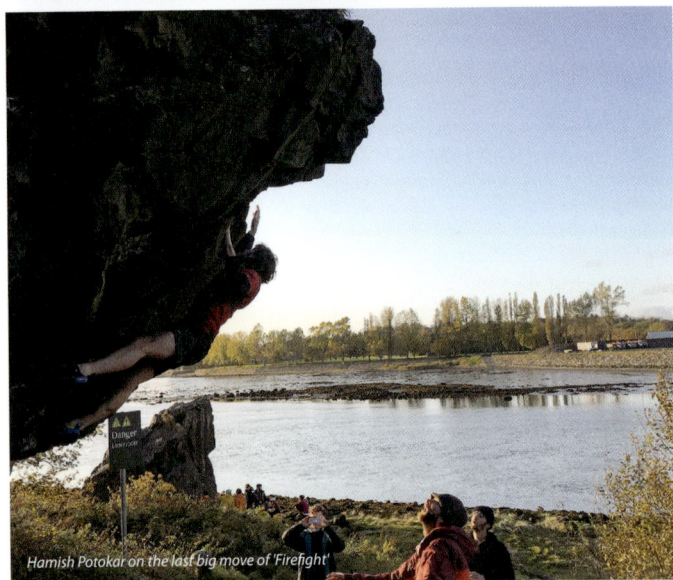

Hamish Potokar on the last big move of 'Firefight'

SECTOR 5: GORILLA CAVE

The black, smoke-stained cave of the Eagle Boulder. All problems finish up the top slab which can be very green and damp after rain. Note: it is possible one of these problems was climbed as an old aid route in the 1960s by Brian Shields, Michael Connolly, & G. McKenzie, called *All the King's Horses* (A4, Severe). Brian Shields' description for this was: 'Start at the cave at the front of the boulder. Come out under the roof and up the nose, all on expansion bolts (now removed). Make a hard move onto the slab and continue to the top.' This may have been an early aid ascent of *High Flyer*, but this is unconfirmed. Projects and link-ups remain to be done: a near-completed project as of 2020 starts from the prop-bloc of *Pressure* and presses right to the hanging start holds on *Gorilla*, with a prospective finish up *Gorilla*, or up *King Kong,* all of which will give big numbers.

▢   a. **High Flyer**   6c

From the right side of the rocky ledge in the cave, position yourself carefully and make a committing jump up right to the chalky flat hold and continue right up jugs to mantle the lip. Some folk use the wee undercut/crimp to aid the lunge for the big hold, whereas the first ascent was achieved with a basketball run-up and dunk. FA John Christie, 1980s.

▢   b. **Smokescreen**   7c

Start at slot holds left of the big flat jug on the lip. Pull on and get a right heel on. Power up left to a hold, then slap right to a tiny ripple on a smooth ramp. Use a left undercut to go right again for the *High Flyer* jug and finish up this. Good spotting and mat placements are essential to protect the nasty fall potential, which makes this problem feel extremely committing. FA Dave MacLeod, 2005.

▢   c. **Pressure**   8b

A new benchmark for Scottish bouldering in 2005. From a heel hook start on the wee pillar at the back of the cave, climb through the big flat layaway and undercut back to the lip. Gain the slot and the flat jug and then finish as for *Smokescreen*. FA Dave MacLeod, 2005.

▢   d. **Firestarter**   8a

Heel-hook the juggy ledge on the cave lip (right hand on flange) and get hands established on poor crimps. Gain a left press hold in the groove and go again for an edge under the niche, then lunge for the slab lip and mantle. FA Dave MacLeod, 2004.

▢   e. **Firefight**   8b

Cave start as for *Pressure* to a bat-hang semi-rest on the flat jugs at the lip, then finish right via *Firestarter*. May be harder than *Pressure* as it finishes up an 8a, but was given the same grade. FA Malcolm Smith, April 2010.

6: GORILLA PROW SECTOR

'Gorilla' in the 90s © Guy Robertson

SECTOR 6: GORILLA PROW

The sharp nose of the Eagle Boulder. A number of variations climb through and around the original problem. All are superb exemplars of Dumbarton bouldering.

☐ a. **Gorilla** 6b+

Pull on at twin crimps on the face and crank up to the right-facing layaway. Match this and then ape up left to the jugs on the lip. Rock over onto the slab using a hold up and right. FA Pete Greenwell, 1978, via a jump to the layaway. An earlier first ascent in 1978 was done by Pete Whillance, using a shoogly stack of cheat stones.

☐ a1. **Cautious Lip** 6b

As for *Gorilla* but goes direct from the flange to a flat hold on the lip above.

☐ a2. **Mother Glasgow's Starlings** 7b+

Cautious Lip then follow the lip of the Eagle boulder rightwards with increasing height to a finish up *Supinator XL*. FA Steve Richardson, September 2014.

☐ a3. **Gorilla Warfare** 7a+

Gorilla to the lip then make a hard traverse left on bad slopers to an iron-cross move to a hold on the jutting nose and rock over to finish. FA Mike Rudden, 2000.

☐ a4. **Gorilla Hanging Start** 7a

Crouch start at a good left-hand finger-edge under the roof and a low right edge on the face. Pull on and make hard moves out to gain the twin crimps (clever heels) and finish up the original problem. FA Darren Stevenson, 2000.

☐ a5. **Hung Like a Gorilla** 7b

As for *Gorilla Hanging*, but finish via *Gorilla Warfare*. FA Peter Roy, 2015.

☐ a6. **Silverback** 7c

From the *Gorilla* crimps move left to match a poor sloper and gain the incut hold on the arête. Boost for the jug on the nose to finish up *Gorilla*. FA Dave MacLeod, 2001.

☐ b. **Neil's Extension/Gorilla Sit Start** 7b+

The true sit start to *Gorilla*. Sit at a low, sloping front-face crimp facing rightwards and a left-hand cave sidepull. A blind slap to the finger edge under the roof leads through clamping moves into the original problem. FA Neil Busby, 2000.

☐ b1. **Silverback Arête** 7c+

Neil's Extension into *Silverback*. A similar variation called *Silverware* starts via the hanging start and finishes via *Silverback* and *Gorilla Warfare* at the same grade.

☐ b2. **King Kong** 8a

The classic complete link-up of *Neil's Extension* into *Silverback* then *Gorilla Warfare*. Eliminates the big lip jug at the top of *Gorilla*. FA Dave MacLeod, 2002.

7: EAGLE FACE SECTOR

Steve Richardson high on his own 'Supinator XL'

SECTOR 7: EAGLE FACE

The long face extending from the cave to a rock plinth by the tree-stump. Beware, the landing slopes badly and should be padded cleverly, it's a big drop from the lip!

☐ a. **Shin Sekai** 6c+

The wall just right of *Gorilla* from an incut level with the layaway. Pull on and make a large move up left to a hold under the lip and mantle. Used to be a 7b dyno until a hold broke and improved. FA Michael Connor, 1999.

☐ a1. **Nature** 8a+

Sit start under *Gorilla*, left hand on a sharp crimp under the roof and a right hand on a low face/lip hold. Slap into a pair of smooth crimps on the face and heel hook up right through further crimps to snatch for the sharp hold on *Shin Sekai*, then finish up this. FA Hamish Potokar, 2019.

☐ b. **Hoop** 7c

Where the prow meets the ground. Gain a finger-jug and rock over to a crimp on top of the 'ear' feature. Go up and left to a hard lip rockover. FA Dave MacLeod, 2001.

☐ c. **Bingham's Wall** 7b+

Jump to the jug rail and go right to another jug. Gain a tiny right-hand crimp on the face and lunge to the lip. Rock onto the slab. FA Richard Bingham, 1999.

☐ c1. **Ladderman** 7c

Jump to the rail and go to the big jug. A huge, morpho left-hand crank gains a hold under the lip in a wee niche, mantle out. FA Will Atkinson, 2011.

☐ d. **Dressed For Success** 7b+

Jump to jugs on the far left. Traverse the rail right to a crux drop-down at the *Supinator* crack, continue along micro-slopers to gain *2HB* via a difficult press move. FA Dave MacLeod, 1999.

☐ e. **Supinator** 6a+

The central crack-line on the front face. A tricky start leads to better holds to a scary rock-over onto the slab. Aptly-named classic. FA Mark Worsley, 1978. Brian Shields climbed an aid version of this in the 1960s, with three pegs, calling it *The Wee Zipper*.

☐ e1. **Supinator XL** 6b+

A right-hand exit to *Supinator*. At three-quarters height go right to flat crimps and past a flat hold to a jug, then mantle onto the slab. FA Steve Richardson, 2014.

☐ f. **2HB** 6a+

The angular groove left of the tree stump has a nippy move at half height to a triangular undercut, then go up through some good crimps to jugs and a mantle.

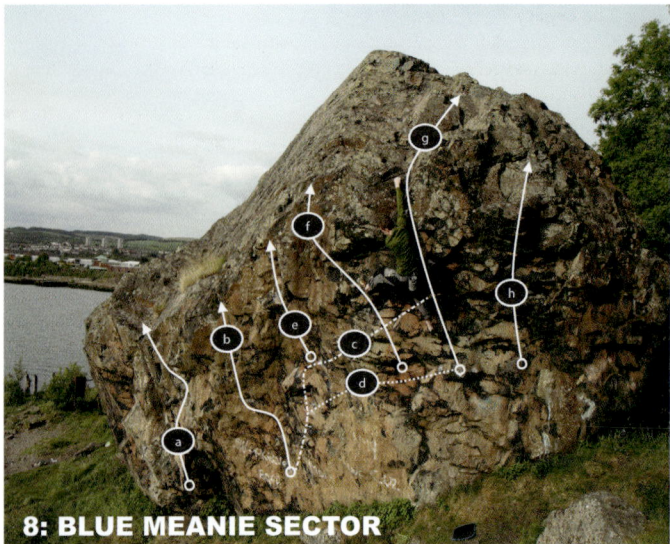

8: BLUE MEANIE SECTOR

Chris Everett on 'Oceans'

❒ g. **The Legacy** 6b+

Start *2HB* but head left immediately to a sloping hold at mid-height. Take an insecure-looking undercling and launch up the bulge on flat holds to an airy finish. FA Steve Richardson, 2014.

❒ h. **A Ford Flash** 7a

The orange groove above the tree. Gain a jug and cross to a crimp and reach up right to a press hold (on *Torino Sun*). A high left-crimp and a hidden right undercut lead to jugs on top. FA Andy Ford, 1980s. A sit start is possible at the same grade.

SECTOR 8: BLUE MEANIE

This is the orange overhanging wall which goes uphill from the tree stump and rock plinth to the descent ledges. Pad out the uneven landings.

❒ a. **Torino Sun** 6b

A modern classic. Step left off the plinth to a right-hand press to a left sidepull, go up right and then stretch or dyno up left to juggy ledges. FA Steve Richardson, 2006.

❒ b. **Oceans** 7c

The orange scoop from the crack holds, twisting left to an undercut. From here step left and cross through to a sloping crimp, gain holds above and commit to a protruding edge up and left. FA Dave MacLeod, 2001.

❒ b1. **Sea Bed** 7c+

Sit start in the short crack at the start of the *1990 Traverse* then climb into *Oceans*. FA Chris Everett, 2013.

❒ c. **1990 Traverse** 7b

Sit start under the *Oceans* groove and layback up a vague crack. Traverse up and right on high crimps to a large flat hold. Continue rightwards to join *Blue Meanie*. FA Andy Gallagher, 1990.

❒ d. **2016 Traverse** 7b+

Start as for *1990* but traverse lower on a series of sloping edges, tiny crimps and poor footholds to reach *Blue Meanie*. FA Simon Smith, 2016.

❒ e. **Snappy** 6b+

Right of *Oceans*. Pounce to a sharp jug hold up and left of the *1990* crimp (committing). Layback the slot above and go right. FA Andy Gallagher, 1996.

❒ f. **Yappy** 6b+

Start 1m left of *Blue Meanie*, heading direct to a large undercling. Use this to yard up left to a distant jug, then a straightforward finish direct. FA John Christie, 1990s.

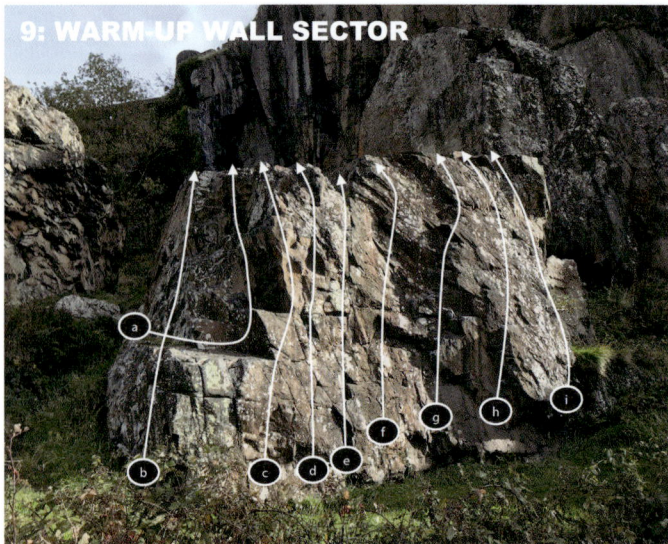

9: WARM-UP WALL SECTOR

A young Tom Richardson high on 'Ungava'

◻ g. **Blue Meanie**   5

A Dumby lesson in commitment! This classic problem takes the angular overhanging wall above the descent path slabs. Twist up to a large right-facing layaway niche and travel nervously left through hidden jugs to pull over the high lip.

◻ h. **PTO**   4+

The high black bulge just right of *Blue Meanie*, with undercut reaches to reluctant jugs. FA (direct) J. Gardner & Neil Macniven, 1960s. The first ascent gained the problem by a leftward traverse from the slabs (FA B. Shields & M. Connolly, 1960s).

SECTOR 9: WARM-UP WALL

This is the pleasant, sea-facing vertical wall over a flat landing, underneath the higher boulder of Home Rule. Walk-off descents.

◻ a. **Beginner's Luck**   1

The left ledges, climb down the shelf from the path, then step up the blocky corner.

◻ b. **Monday Wall**   1+

The left ledges but take the short north wall over the path via jugs to the lip.

◻ c. **Left Edge**   3

The left arête of the wall from the front, a tricky step on leads to a right-hand pinch and left-hand jugs.

◻ d. **Tuesday Wall**   3+

The left wall between the edge and crack, via pocket above the pinch to gain the jugs.

◻ e. **Friday's Fill**   3

The crack on the left wall is a classic warm-up. Mantle out onto ledges. FA Brian Shields & Michael Connolly, 1960s. Originally given a 'severe' grade in big boots.

◻ f. **Thursday Wall**   5+

Eliminate. Start right of the crack, step on to the wall at jugs, then take a left-hand press to stand on the jugs. Climb the higher blank wall via crimps, using no jugs.

◻ g. **Friar's Mantle**   4+

The stepped groove and sloping ledges in the middle of the wall. A puzzling move at half-height provides the crux, some use a wide slopey pinch. FA Neil Macniven, 1960s. A dyno version eliminating the slopers is 6a.

◻ h. **Ungava**   4+

The wall right of *Friar's Mantle* from the jug ledge. Gain a pocket and sidepull on the wall then crank up right to crimps and easier ground, without using the right edge. FA Neil Macniven, 1960s. A dyno version missing the sidepull and pocket is 6a.

10: VALHALLA

John Hutchinson contemplating 'Valhalla'

❒ i. **Right Edge** 3+

A tricky start at the right-hand overlap on the wall to the layback edge on the right.

❒ j. **Warm-Up Traverse** 4

Left Edge to *Right Edge* using the easiest line of jugs and crimps. A lower 6a version keeps under chin height, as low as possible, with the crux just right of the crack, whichever direction you take. Add a grade each traverse till you drop off.

SECTOR 10: VALHALLA

The bold, high walls of the Home Rule bloc facing the main crag face. The descent is 'The Beast' arête which feels easier going up than downclimbing. They are not very popular but remain impressively bold challenges from the 60s.

❒ a. **The Switch** 5

Start as for *Valhalla* at the join of the boulders. Step down and left onto the hanging slab and climb the groove between *Valhalla* and *The Whip* (further left). The FA was described as 'extremely delicate' and climbed in Vibram boots: no excuses then! A later variation takes the top right bulge. FA Neil Macniven & Brian Shields, 1963.

❒ b. **Valhalla** 4

The committing shallow groove above the join of the two boulders. Bridge up over the chasm to a big sidepull jug, then finish directly up the edge of the thin slabby groove via a high-step and small holds. FA Brian Shields & Michael Connolly, 1960s.

❒ c. **The Beauty** 4

The slabby wall and overlaps left of *The Beast*, right of *Valhalla*. Climb the slab to the overlap then trend right technically to step into the grooves.

❒ d. **Orange Wall** 6a

Sit start at polished lip finger slopers just left of *The Beast* arête, slap up right to jugs and rock left onto the orange slab. Long reaches up and left gain poor edges and a standing position to better holds right of *The Beauty,* finish up this or *The Beast*.

❒ e. **The Beast** 3

The highball juggy black arête at the back is also the descent from this boulder, taken on the cleaner *Valhalla* side. FA Neil Macniven, 1960s.

❒ f. **Einherjar** 6b+

Start at the *Hokku* jug under the roof. Slap out to the lip of the hanging bulge. A tricky move leftwards gains a sidepull/undercut onto the base of the slab. Tiptoe delicately up and left to gain the jug of *Valhalla* and finish up this. FA Stewart Brown 2010.

❒ g. **Skin Deep** 6b+

Starts as for *Einherjar* and gains the good hold at the base of the slab. Break rightwards and up to join *The Beauty* and finish up this. FA Stewart Brown, 2010.

The Beast

11: THE BEAST SLABS

Eleanor Hopkins on 'Encore Une Fois'

SECTOR 11: THE BEAST SLABS

Often very green and mossy, these slabs need a good civic cleaning before ascents.

☐ a. **The Brute** 4

Start just right of *The Beast* and pull off the ground into the wee hanging groove using tricky foot edges, finish up *The Beast*. A sit start from the left is 5+.

☐ b. **Valkyrie** 4+

Just right of *The Brute* is a hanging orange slab on the left side of the bulge above the smaller prop rock. Bridge or layback up into this to gain the slab and finish up this via a ledge and high left groove. FA Brian Shields & Michael Connolly, 1960s.

☐ c. **Encore Une Fois** 6c+

Step on right at *Pas Encore* to the big jug, then hang this footless and traverse left round the nose. Use left slopers to slap for a crimp to beg onto the slab. FA John Watson, 2013.

☐ d. **Pas Encore** 5

Above the larger of the two prop rocks is a groove right of the bulge. Step on the right side of the prop boulder and pull steeply over left on a foot-jug to gain slopers on the slab, finish straight up the slab. FA Neil Macniven, 1960s.

☐ e. **Crimp!** 6b+

The jutting nose on its left side. From a standing position on the right of the prop bloc, gain a slot hold under the roof, then flat holds above. Bed down on a crimp above and just left of the arête and top out directly. FA Steve Richardson, 2000.

☐ f. **More Chicken** 7a+

An eliminate taking the arête left of the *Head Butt* groove. From the right edge of the larger prop block gain a triangular slot hold under the sharp arête and slap up the left side of this direct. Holds left as for *Crimp!* are out. FA Dave Macleod, 1999.

SECTOR 12: MUGSY ROOF

The cave roof leading underneath the boulder has a ramped northern lip with classic power problems, and probably too many link-ups, which can make things confusing!

☐ a. **Head Butt** 7a

Start standing on the block and pull into the corner right of the nose, using the left arête of the groove. A head-jam was used originally. FA Andy Gallagher, 1993.

☐ a1. **Butt Head** 7a+

Head Butt but sit start on the prop block, hands in the slot. Move up to the lip into *Head Butt*. Easier for the tall. FA Alex Gorham & Jonathan Bean, 2011.

12: MUGSY ROOF SECTOR

Sam Scriven on 'Mugsy'

❏ a2 **Chicken Butt**   7a+
Butt Head into *More Chicken*. FA Alan Cassidy, 2015.

❏ b. **Malky**   7b
Hang the starting jug of *Mugsy* but then take the sloping lip crimp with the right
hand and go direct to the sloping shelf (heel-toe lock). A more modern method is
to swing hard left to a frustratingly distant slopey sidepull (just below and left of the
sloping shelf), then gain the shelf. Get standing on the shelf direct without the *Mugsy*
jug out right. FA Dave MacLeod 2000.

❏ b1. **Malky Sit Start**   7b+
Starting as for *Mugsy Sit* on crimps, gain the original problem of *Malky*.

❏ b2. **Dagger**   7b+
Stand start to *Malky*, then finish up *Head Butt*.

❏ b3. **Malky Traverse**   7b+
From the left of the cave, traverse the handrail right and finish up *Malky*.

❏ b4. **Malkied**   7c
Mugsy Traverse into *Malky,* then from the sloping shelf finish via *Head Butt*. FA Chris
Houston, 2010.

❏ b5. **Malky's Chicken**   7b+
Malkied but stay low under the prow into *More Chicken*. FA Euan McFadyen, 2015.

❏ b6. **Glasgow Kiss**   7c+
Spam into the starting jug of *Mugsy* to finish up *Malky*. FA Will Atkinson, 2010.

❏ b7. **Spam Dagger**   8a
Start as for *Spam* into *Malky,* then finish into the groove of *Head Butt*. FA Will
Atkinson, 2011.

❏ c. **Mugsy**   7a
The centre of the face from the handrail jugs. Jump start to a high right sloper, sort
feet and gain a left undercut, or the lip crimp, then throw for a distant jug. Finish left
or more easily right into the *Mestizo* groove. FA Dave Cuthbertson, 1983.

❏ c1. **Mugsy Hanging Start**   7a+
AKA *Mugsy Static*. Hand-match the big lip jug, making use of heels, left or right, then
crank up to the right-hand sloper and lunge for the high jug.

❏ c2. **Mugsy Sit Start**   7b
Sit start from the twin crimps on the steep roof of the cave. A left toe-hook eases
the lunge to the jug. From here enter the hanging start.

12: MUGSY VARIATIONS

Thom Davies on 'Mugstizo' © Beth Chalmers

❐ **c3. Spam** 7c

A very low but classic sit start to *Mugsy*. Sit deep under the L-shaped sharp flake and twist to the poor twin crimps of *Mugsy Sit Start*, then slap for the jugs and finish up *Mugsy*. No block for feet. FA Dave MacLeod, 2002.

❐ **c4. Mestugso** 7b

Sit start *Mugsy* at the crimps to the jugs and right traverse into *Mestizo* via slopers with a crux redpoint move to the arête.

❐ **c5. Knowledge Is Power** 7b+

From *Mugsy Sit Start* traverse right round the *Mestizo* arête to reverse the *Home Rule Low Traverse*, finishing up *Home Rule*. A real toughie. FA Dave MacLeod, 1998.

❐ **c6. Dweller** 7a

Sit start the cave a little left of the *Mugsy Sit* crimps, at a good incut hold. Use the long crimp of *Spam* and gain the juggy ledge (foot on the jammed block on right is allowed). Drop off here. Continue up *Mugsy* for 7b+. FA Mike Tweedley, 2002.

❐ **c7. Set in Motion** 7c+

Sit start at the same incut crimp of *Dweller* but without the prop rock for feet. Crimp through tiny holds directly upwards to the *Mugsy Traverse* slopers and hold the cut loose swing. Finish up *Mugsy*. FA Dave MacLeod, 2007.

❐ **c8. Mugsly** 7b+

Eliminate. *Mugsy Static* but from the high right sloper go direct left to the shelf of *Malky* and finish up this.

❐ **c9. Mugslife** 7c

Mugsly but finish via *Head Butt*. FA Euan MacFadyen, 2014.

❐ **c10. Spamsly** 7c+

Mugsly but via the sit start of *Spam*. FA Jack McKechnie, 2019.

❐ **d. Mugsy Traverse** 7b

Start sitting on a small boulder on the left side of the cave. Pull on footless and traverse the line of sloping jugs rightwards into the hanging start jugs, using a cunning heel-toe lock to move into the original problem. FA Andy Gallagher, 1993.

❐ **d1. Mugsy Traverse Extension** 7b+

From a large, sloping hold far back in the cave, traverse out to join *Mugsy Traverse*.

❐ **d2. Hokku** 8a

Start in the depths of the cave at a spiky jug under *Valhalla,* by Sucker's boulder. Climb backwards with toe-hooks into the cave via small crimps and sloping pinches to escape out right to *Mugsy Traverse Extension*. FA Dave MacLeod, 2007.

Alan Cassidy on the long convoluted journey that is 'Sosho' © Helen Cassidy

12: MESTIZO VARIATIONS

❑ d3. **Sosho** 8a+

Hokku, with an extended master sequence from *The Whip Sit Start*. Upside-down climbing leads into the cave proper to gain the *Hokku* starting jug. From here continue through the *Hokku* crux into *Mugsy Traverse*. FA Dave MacLeod, 2007.

❑ e. **Mestizo** 6a

The arête. Swing up left to a good flattie, then use an undercut or slopey pinch to gain a good hold on the arête. Step into the groove to finish. FA Gary Latter, 1980.

❑ e1. **Mestizo Sit Start** 7a+

The overhanging sit start of the sharp arête. Crawl in close under the arête and take an upside-down straddle position. From a slopey right-hand layaway and a left-hand cave crimp slap up left to the ledge, then gain the good crimps on the arête. Finish up the original problem. FA Dave MacLeod, 2000.

❑ e2. **Mestizo Direct** 7a

From the starting crimp-match of *Mestizo*, boost directly to the jug and climb the right side of the wall for two moves to rock into the *Mestizo* groove nearer the top.

❑ e3. **Mestizo Traverse** 7b

Start *Mugsy Traverse* but continue all the way to a crux sequence to gain holds on *Mestizo* via a tricky 'cup hold' crux on the arête. FA Andy Gallagher,1997.

❑ e4. **Mugstizo** 7b+

Sit start *Mestizo* but move left to gain the starting handrail jug of *Mugsy* via difficult clamping. Finish up this with a clever sequence negotiating the static version of *Mugsy*. FA Stewart Brown, 2009. A higher traverse section is easier at 7b.

❑ e5. **Mestizo Traverse Extension** 7b+

Starting as for *Mugsy Traverse Extension* but finishing up *Mestizo*.

❑ e6. **More Malkstizo** 7a

Start up *Head Butt* and then reverse *Malkied* into the sloper, go across *Mugsy* to top out up *Mestizo*. FA Alan Cassidy, 2015.

❑ e7. **Nice and Sleazy** 7c+

Quality modern link up starting up *Mestizo Sit Start* left along the shelf to the jugs then continue left to finish up *Malky*. FA Will Atkinson, 2010.

❑ e8. **Nice and Sleazier** 7c+

Home Rule Low Traverse but continue into *Nice and Sleazy*. FA Will Atkinson, 2010.

❑ e9. **Eazy Sleazy** 7c+

Nice and Sleazier into *Malkied*. Nothing easy about it. FA Dan Walker, 2011.

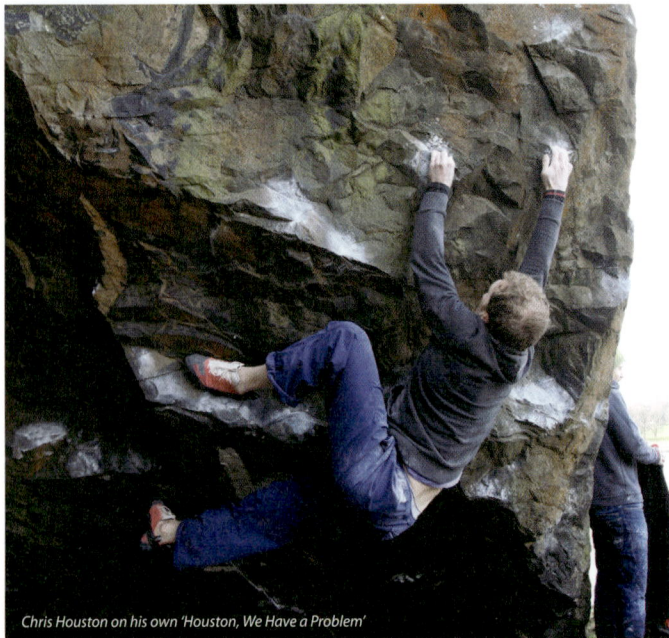
Chris Houston on his own 'Houston, We Have a Problem'

13: HOME RULE SECTOR

❑ e10. **Thoroughbred** 7c+

Long right to left link-up. Start as for *Mestizo Sit Start* and climb left to climb up *Malky,* but finish as for *Head Butt.* FA Alex Gorham, 2010.

❑ e11. **Malky's Sleazy Chicken** 8a

Even longer. Climb *Thoroughbred* but finish up *More Chicken.* FA Euan McFadyen, July 2015.

❑ e12. **Houston, We Have a Problem** 7b

Start on sloping ledge holds just right of *Mugsy,* gain the *Mugsy* sloper with the left hand and finish into *Mestizo.* FA Chris Houston, 2009.

❑ e13. **Power Relation** 7b

Mestizo Sit Start into *Home Rule,* reversing the moves on H*ome Rule Low Traverse.* FA Jack McKechnie, 2018.

SECTOR 13: HOME RULE

The flat front face of the boulder looking out to the River Leven.

❑ a. **Physical Graffiti** 6b

The highball line of crimps straight up the main face of the Home Rule boulder. Start left of the centre and make a difficult move to gain a good high edge. High-step to further edges and nervously step rightwards to a pleasantly generous crimp below the lip, a good place to get scared, then mantle out with care. FA Gary Latter, 1980.

❑ a1. **Art Attack** 7b

SS *Mestizo* and link this into *Physical Graffiti.* Gives you a nice forearm pump for the highball section! FA 'Cobra' Stuart Lyall, 2013.

❑ a2. **Spray On** 7b

Home Rule Low into the *Art Attack* link to *Physical Graffiti.* FA Simon Smith, 2015.

❑ b. **Home Rule** 6a

The central wall from the rail, through a blunt pinch or big rock-over to the higher handrail, traverse right to finish up via the arête or alternatively finish direct.

❑ b1. **Devolution** 6b+

A right-hand version of *Home Rule.* Sit start in the niche to the right, crimp up to stand on a foot-ledge. Gain the pinch with the left hand, finish by the ledges and arête of *Home Rule.* FA John Watson, 2000.

❑ c. **Home Rule High Traverse** 6b

Start as for *Home Rule,* but traverse left to join the *Mestizo* arête jug via small edges from the high handrail, then turn the corner and rock into the groove.

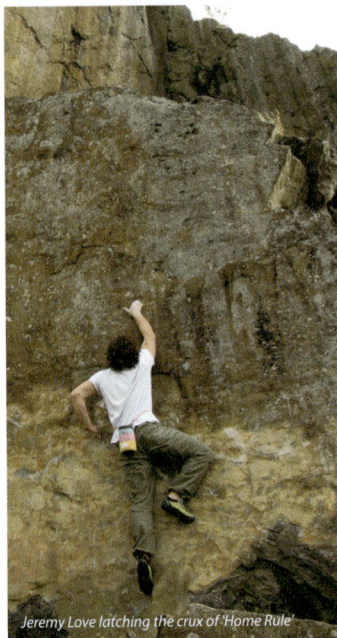

Jeremy Love latching the crux of 'Home Rule'

Andy Gallagher on 'Royal Arête' © Guy Robertson

14: ROUTE ROYALE SECTOR

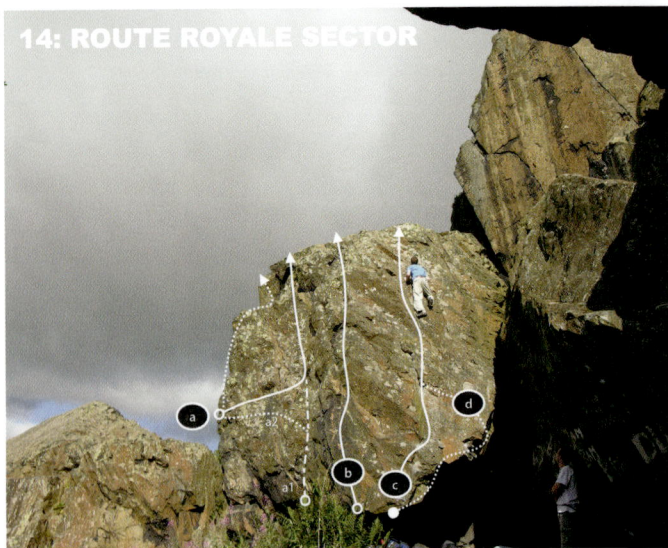

❑ d. **Home Rule Low Traverse**   7a+

Super-technical classic. From the arête of *Presence*, traverse low left to join *Mestizo*. Harder than the original 7a after a hold broke. FA Andy Gallagher, 1995.

❑ e. **Bob's Problem**   6a

Eliminate. From the crimpy rail just left of the *Presence* arête, gain the sloper left of the arête with the right hand, then up to the higher rail. FA Robert Ewan, 2000.

❑ f. **Presence**   5+

The unnerving right arête leans out over the drop before the handrail ... careful!

SECTOR 14: ROUTE ROYALE

The highball grooved wall above the sloping grass right of the rock-step of the *Home Rule* wall. All problems feel more like E2 or E3 solos.

❑ a. **Route Royale**   5+

One of the boldest problems from the 1960s, given a grade of *Very Severe*. The original came in from the Home Rule ledge to the left, swinging rightwards into the fault. Climb up the fault to a sloping shelf on the left and gain the top. FA Neil Macniven, 1960s. Can be climbed direct at 6a from the grass slope.

❑ a1. **Route Royale SS**   6c

The sit start into the *Route Royale* groove from the grass slope uses an undercut in the cave, pressing left, then gains the niche groove above. Finish via the original.

❑ a2. **Chicken Royale**   6c

A variation which sit starts and laybacks up the left side of the central groove but travels left to the arête jug, turning into and finishing up *Presence*.

❑ a3. **Route Royale Wall Traverse**   6b

Step on as for *The Whip* but go hard left across the groove, gain some height and take ledges left to *Home Rule* wall step off, or finish up *Presence*.

❑ a4. **Royale Beauty**   6a

From the rest position in the groove on *Route Royale* head straight up via a positive crimp and a number of slopers, possibly using a small finger lock below the overlap. Another highball. FA Steve Richardson, 2007.

❑ b. **Royal Arête**   6b

The arête taken direct, trending right of *Route Royale* at the niche in the arête. Highball, take care. FA Andy Gallagher, 1996.

❑ c. **The Whip**   5+

The highball slabby grooves right of *Royal Arête*. Pull on to jugs then tiptoe directly

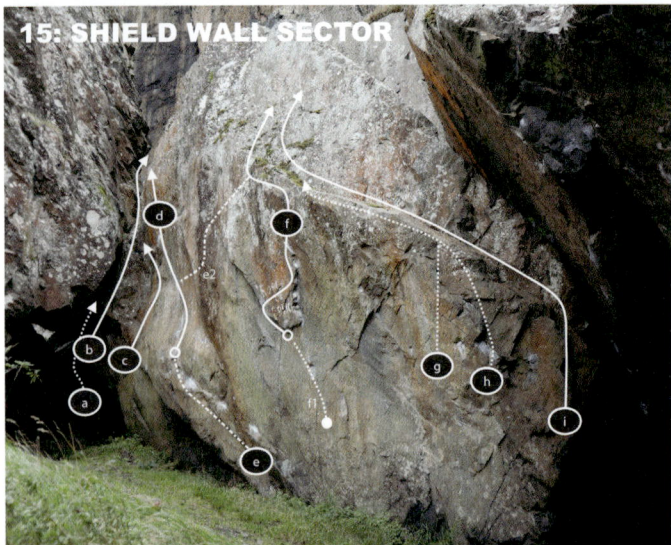

15: SHIELD WALL SECTOR

Pete Roy on 'Totality' © Stewart Brown

Ben Pritchard on 'The Shield' © Tim Morozzo

up to a nervy escape-step left near the top to good holds. Finishing directly over the bulge is even scarier, give yourself a brave pill and another grade.

❒ d. **The Whip Sit Start** 6c

Very different from its parent problem, requiring an aggressive approach. Sit start on low flat holds at the base of *Royal Arête* to a lunging traverse right to a large sidepull, gain a sharp crimp on the hanging slab and rock out left to a distant jug. Finish as for *The Whip* (or wimp out as for *P.S.*). A direct stand version is 6a+.

SECTOR 15: SUCKER'S BOULDER

The squeezed-in, leaning, wall between Home Rule and B.N.I. boulders. The showpiece is the ultra-classic *Shield* problem.

❒ a. **Cave Route** 6b

Sit start the short arête left of *Toto* and climb left into the cave and up through the squeeze gap. More caving than climbing.

❒ a1. **Cave Route Right** 6a+

Sit start as for *Cave Route* but head right into the light and up to the *Toto* jug.

❒ b. **P.S.** 3

The cramped chimney or groove between the Home Rule and Sucker's boulders is a bit of a traditional struggle. Start at jugs and use anything on both boulders.

❒ c. **Unnamed (AKA Andy's Problem)** 6b

A good problem from directly below the *Toto* finishing jug. Stand start via small holds and use a shallow pocket left of the crack to get established in the groove and gain the *Toto* jug direct. FA Andy Gallagher, 1992.

❒ d. **Toto** 6a+

The slanting crack in the scoop on the left is a technical delight. Get established in the crack via polished footholds. Move up the crack to a high right-hand press crimp, allowing a nervy cross-step left to a jug. Finish trending left. FA Gary Latter, 1980.

❒ d1. **Toto Right-Hand** 6b+

Get established in the crack but keep right of the crack, using the right-hand crimp on *Totality* to gain the crimp above and up to the ledges.

❒ e. **Toto Sit Start** 7a

A classic crimper. Sit start low right as far right as possible at small crimps under *The Shield*, in a cross-handed position. Traverse up and left to join the crack of *Toto*. FA Cameron Phair, 1994.

Eilidh Milne on 'Toto'

❒ e1. **Toto Traverse** 7a+

Follow *Toto Sit Start* to the good hold at the start of the crack. Make a very long reach up left to a variety of holds depending on your height and continue to finish up *P.S.* FA Andy Gallagher, 1996. A lower finish may or may not be possible.

❒ e2. **Totality** 7b+

A popular and technical problem. Climb *Toto Sit Start* and get established in the crack, reach right across the wall to a poor crimp, drop down to a sloping left-hand hold, then a crux sequence right leads to a mantle. FA M. Casey, 2003.

❒ e3. **Totalled** 7b

A satisfying and natural stand-up version of *Totality,* if you can't link the sit start.

❒ e4. **Toto Sit Start Direct** 7a+

Start as for *Toto Sit Start* but once a standing position has been reached in the *Toto* crack, finish up *Toto Right Hand*. FA Dave Macleod, 2009.

❒ f. **The Shield** 7b+

A famous Dumby power problem. Clamp the shield feature anywhere you can. Pull on with poor footholds, then lunge for the sloping lip and mantle. The outlawed 'undercut method', due to a broken hold, may make it feel easier (but is used to link the sit start method). FA Malcolm Smith, 1994.

❒ f1. **The Shield Sit Start** 7c

Sit start at the pocket and gain the wee broken undercut at the bottom left of *The Shield*, allowed for the sit, then gain the original problem. FA Dave Redpath, 1997.

❒ f2. **The Shield Right-Hand** 7a+

From *The Shield* undercut and a sidepull way out right of the shield feature, escape right to the lip, then back left to finish as for *The Shield*. FA Neil Busby, 1999

❒ f3. **The Shield Right-Hand Sit Start** 7b

Start as for *The Shield Sit Start* but go right to the right-hand 'escape' version. FA Will Atkinson, 2009.

❒ g. **Power Pockets** 6c

The twin pockets at chin-height on the right allow a one-move slap to the sloping ledge, mantle out.

❒ g1. **Power Pockets Sit Start** 7c

Using two low sloping crimps, gain *Power Pockets* and finish up this. FA Dave Macleod, 2000.

❒ g2. **Redpath's Problem** 7b

Use the left-hand power pocket with the right hand, and a left hand on a pinch out

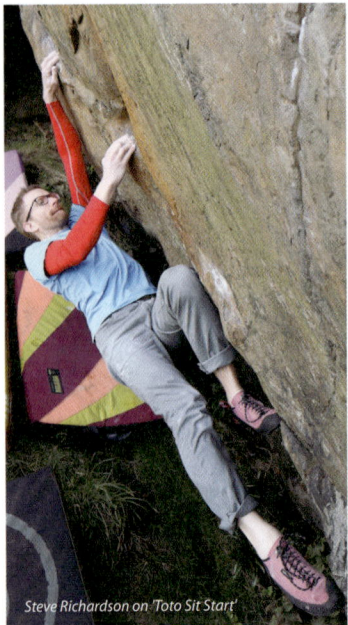

Steve Richardson on 'Toto Sit Start'

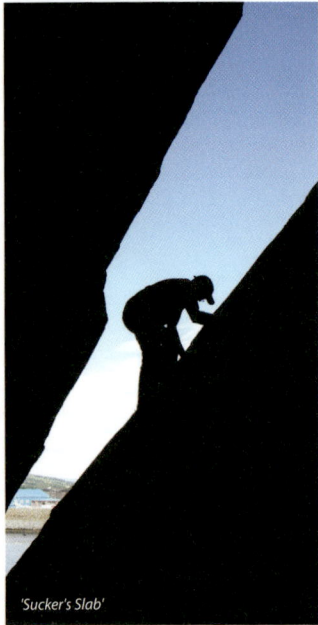

'Sucker's Slab'

16: SUCKER'S SLAB SECTOR

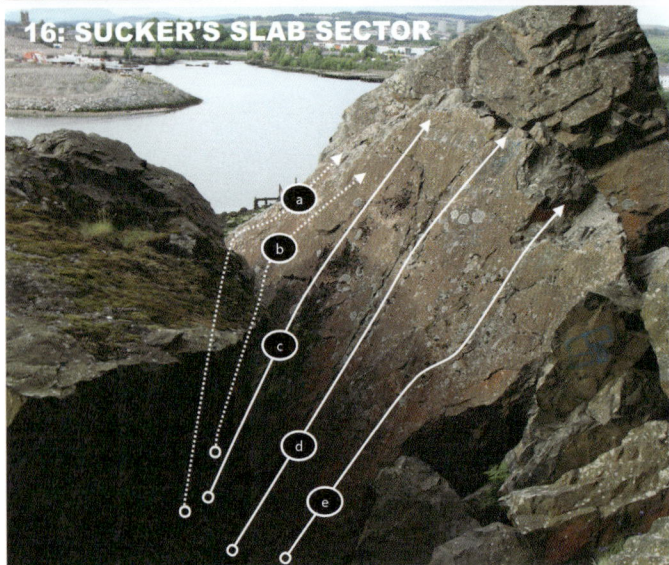

left, step on and slap for an edge above the ledge sloper (under a small pocket). Pull over. FA Dave Redpath, 1998.

❒ h. **The Railings** 6b+

The popular hand-traverse of the slopey *Snooker Shelf* ledge. From the large pockets on the arête, pounce high left to a sloper edge on the lip, match, then traverse hard left, often footless, to finish with a mantle above *The Shield*. FA Mike Conner, 1999.

❒ h1. **The Railings Sit Start** 6c

Sit start at the arête on the right and climb up left to join *The Railings*.

❒ h2. **Off the Rails** 6c+

The Railings but continuing to the *Toto* jug and step into the gap at *P.S.*

❒ i. **Snooker Shelf** 4

Climb up from the far right corner of the face, by the walkthrough cave, and tiptoe left along the ramp to finish up a groove left of *The Shield*. FA Neil Macniven, 1960s.

❒ i1. **Kneebar** 6a+

Sit start *Snooker Shelf* just left of the wee jammed boulder at a big sidepull, possibly using a kneebar, and gain the original problem. FA Andy Gallagher 1999.

❒ i2. **Kneebar Extension** 6c+

Kneebar into *Off the Rails*.

SECTOR 16: SUCKER'S SLAB

❒ a. **Mosca** 3+

The left arête of the slab, gained by squeezing along from the back corridor behind the B.N.I. boulder. May need a good clean like other routes on this slab. FA Brian Shields, 1960s.

❒ b. **Antimatter** 4

Eliminate smearing up the slab right of *Mosca* without using the left arête.

❒ c. **Sucker's Slab** 4+

The thin slab left of the *Volpone* crack, straight up the centre on friction holds. FA Neil Macniven, 1960s.

❒ d. **Volpone Crack** 3

The intermittent crack on polished holds and foot smears.

❒ e. **Smear Test** 3

The slab on the right of the crack, off a pillar stone by the right arête, not using anything in the *Volpone* crack. Gain good higher holds via smearing. Pad the landing.

17: WALKTHROUGH SECTOR NORTH

Dave MacLeod on 'The Perfect Crime'

SECTOR 17: B.N.I. WALKTHROUGH

The walkthrough cave under the B.N.I boulder. Big enough for humans, but not with boulder mats! The cave runs from a northerly aspect to the south roof under the slabs. Some of the link-ups have had few repeats and grades are difficult to calibrate due to their length as extended traverses into various straight-ups. The project of reversing *Perfect Crime* into *Chahala Sit Start* will certainly provide a big number.

❐ a. **Chahala**　　　　　　　　　　　　5+

Jump start the three 'campus' edges on the hanging north wall above the walkthrough cave. Finish by stepping right round onto the Pongo boulder. Ground erosion is making the initial jump quite a challenge.

❐ a1. **Chahala Sit Start Easy**　　　　　　　6a

Sit start on wee boulder jammed in the chimney, pull up to arête jugs, then bridge and twist up to the campus jugs using holds on Sucker's Boulder as well, finish up the original problem.

❐ a2. **Chahala Sit Start**　　　　　　　　8b

Sit start the arête by the prop boulder in the cave tunnel and clamp up this to join the original problem. No use of the prop boulder. Desperate backwards throwing and hard clamping. FA Dave MacLeod, 2007.

❐ b. **The Perfect Crime**　　　　　　　　8a+

Start from a crouching left-hand sidepull and a right-hand slot at the left edge of the roof. Low contortions and inversions rightwards lead to a knee-bar shake-out at the wee hanging ramp where *Sabotage* starts. Now just finish up this if you have anything left. Hard for the grade. FA Dave MacLeod, 2005.

❐ b1. **Perfect Crime Extension**　　　　　　8b

Start as for *The Serum of Sisyphus* and finish up *Sabotage*. FA Malcolm Smith, 2010.

❐ b2. **The Serum of Sisyphus**　　　　　　8a+

Start matching on the nose of the Sucker's Boulder at two good holds, press right onto the B.N.I. boulder and span out to join *Perfect Crime* and follow this to the first kneebar on the spike. Continue round the corner to climb the *Good Nicks* crack to finish at the halfway jugs. FA Malcolm Smith, 2007.

❐ b3. **The Crime of Sisyphus**　　　　　　8a

The easiest of these variations but still hard! Start as for *The Perfect Crime* but follow the *Serum* finish round the corner and up *Good Nicks* to the ledges.

❐ b4. **Grand Tour**　　　　　　　　　　8b

The *Perfect Crime Extension* but finishing up *Le Saboteur* instead. Very long, very pumpy and very hard. FA Malcolm Smith, 2010.

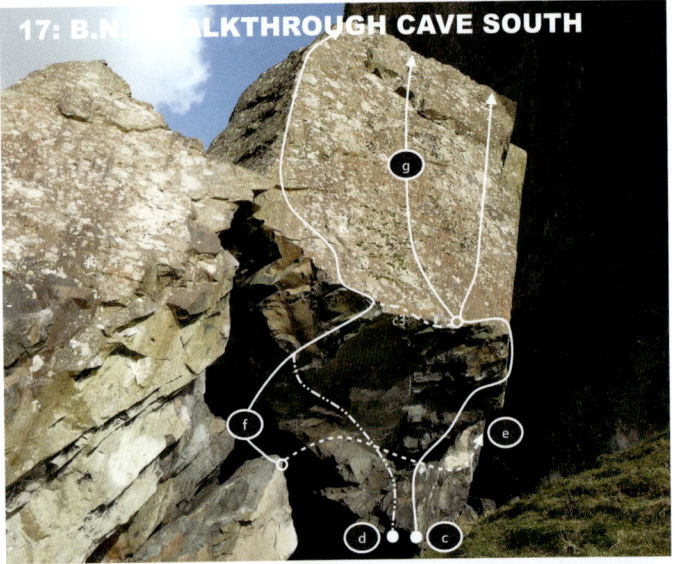

17: B.N.I. WALKTHROUGH CAVE SOUTH

Malcolm Smith on 'Sanction'

❑ b5. **Gutbuster** 8b+

One of Scotland's very hardest problems. Start via *The Serum of Sisyphus* and follow this right to the kneebar rest on a spike at the base of the tiny hanging slab. Gain as much recovery here as possible before finishing up *Sanction* onto the slabs. Finish up *Imposter Arête* to celebrate. FA Malcolm Smith, 2008.

❑ c. **Sabotage** 8a

Sit start at the western entrance to the cave walkthrough, right of the wee hanging slab, at two pinches. Undercut or kneebar backwards to gain a poor right-hand sloper, with a foot jam in the crack. Use arête holds to make a tricky and initially horizontal heel-rockover sequence onto the slab. FA Dave MacLeod, 2003.

❑ c1. **Sabotaged** 8a

As for *Sabotage* but move left to finish via *B.N.I. Direct*. FA Will Atkinson, 2011.

❑ c2. **Le Tour de Technique** 7b+

From the right arête of *Sabotage*, make a difficult move to gain the base of *B.N.I. Direct*. Using unlikely holds continue leftwards to finish up *Very Ape*. Intimidating. FA Mike Lee, 2010.

❑ c3. **Le Saboteur** 8a+

Sabotage into *Le Tour de Technique* via a devious sequence. FA Malcolm Smith, 2010.

❑ d. **Sanction** 8b

The flying roof at the south entrance to the walkthrough B.N.I. cave. SS opposite the wee tunnel bloc, at holds on the left of a small hanging slab, and crank up into the flat holds above making use of a right heel on a small spike. From a high left spike, make a crux lunge to the inset hold below the lip and finish onto the slab via *Very Ape*. FA Dave MacLeod, 2007.

❑ e. **Elbow Basher** 7b+

Match holds on the tunnel's pointed bloc (under the Pongo bloc descent), step down and across to the wee slab of the start of *Sabotage*, then, using holds on *Sanction*, finish round the corner (high or low) via *Good Nicks*. FA Dave MacLeod, 1997.

❑ f. **Very Ape** 6c

Start up the descent hole then pull right on undercuts in the *Sanction* roof to reach round onto the slab of *B.N.I.* and pull on via mono-pockets. Finish up *B.N.I. Slab Direct*. FA Dave MacLeod, 1998.

❑ g. **B.N.I. Direct** 7b+

Stand on the stone plinth and start by hanging two crimps on the lip of the slab. Pull on and make a long morpho reach to a sharp crimp, get established on the slab and finish as for *B.N.I. Slab Direct*. A heel-hook on the lip out left might make this easier for some. FA Malcolm Smith, 1994.

Stewart Brown on 'Good Nicks'

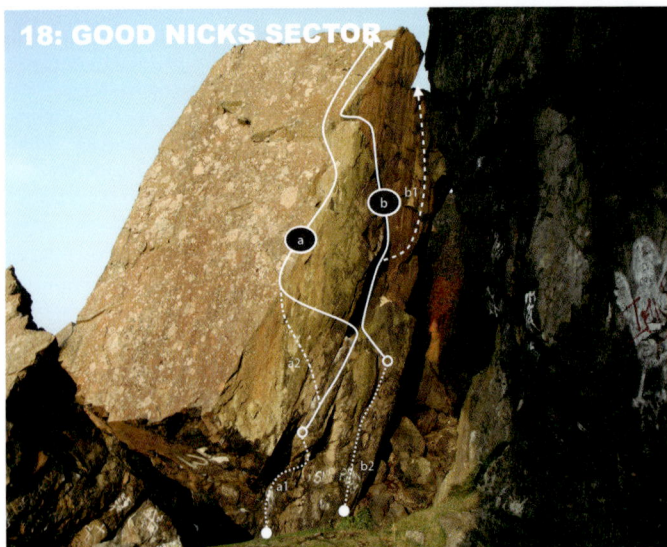

18: GOOD NICKS SECTOR

SECTOR 18: GOOD NICKS

The tall wall of the B.N.I boulder, not a place to have a wobble.

☐ a. **Good Nicks** 6b

A classic old peg crack up the groove right of the hanging B.N.I. slab. Climb the crack right to ledge jugs, then step left and reach for a distant crimp on the edge of the slab. Cross through onto the slab and finish up *Pendulum* arête. FA Willie Todd, 1978.

☐ a1. **Good Nicks Sit Start** 6c

The whitish groove under the old peg crack, starting at two pinches as for *Sabotage*. Subtle body positioning and the odd kneebar makes it easier! Twist into the crack and finish up the original problem.

☐ a2. **You're Nicked** 7b+

The wall direct above the *Good Nicks* crack. From the crack's finger lock, climb the wall via slopey crimps to lunge for the wee hold on the arête, some use a tricky Egyptian. Finish up the slab. FA Dave MacLeod, 2001.

☐ b. **Pendulum** 4

The giant juggy flake above the ledges of *Good Nicks* is another ridiculously bold 60s line. Climb the flake boldly to pull left round the semi-detached block onto the slab. Finish up the right edge. FA Neil MacNiven 1963.

☐ b1. **Revelation** 6a+

A truly committing problem. Climb *Pendulum* into a finger lock in the flake and span right to reach holds at the base of the hanging groove (left of the prow). Climb this on its left side and finish into it to the top. This was given British 5a in an old guide and requires old-school bravado.

☐ b2. **HP** 6b

The eliminate wall and arête. Sit start just right of *Good Nicks* and gain the ledges.

☐ c. **Nadjilation** 6c+

The tall and frightening overhanging wall round the back above the guillotine-edged boulder. Make a crux lunge to the top from a flange. Without protective mats, it may be considered E6! FA Dave MacLeod, 1998.

☐ d. **Sugar Rush** 7b

The cramped sit start to the overhanging arête at the back of B.N.I. boulder beside the *Volpone* crack. Stack mats and clamp hard. FA Dave MacLeod, 2003.

☐ e. **Jump!** (Descent) (5+)

The art of descending: more parkour than bouldering. From the top of the boulder, walk out onto a point of rock opposite the sports wall. Jump to a small ledge opposite, about six feet. It's terrifying, but over quickly.

19: B.N.I. SLABS LEFT

19: B.N.I. SLABS RIGHT

SECTOR 19: B.N.I SLABS

There are two faces of hanging slabs: one on the left of the descent hole is a river-facing slab on the ledge above the descent hole of the Pongo boulder; the other on the right of the descent hole is the high undercut slab facing the Clyde estuary. The higher right slab has a long fall potential, so care is required.

◻ a. **Harvester of Eyes** 3

Climb up the descent hole to the ledge and walk to the *Chahala* side. Climb the open groove via slopey ledges.

◻ b. **Astronomy** 3

The grooved rib on the left of the mezzanine slab is also the descent route. Step off a cracked pillar.

◻ c. **Gratis Rib** 3+

The left edge of the slab beside *Astronomy*, but not using holds on this. Step on right of the cracked pillar. Use crimps on the slab and the left edge to climb direct to the top. Descent is via *Astronomy*.

◻ d. **Deo Gratis** 4+

An excellent slab problem. Climb the central slab left of *Imposter Arête* to an undercut and a committing step up on a tiny foot edge to gain better holds above. FA Neil Macniven, 1960s.

◻ e. **Imposter Arête** 3+

The dramatic right edge arête of the mezzanine slab above the descent route is straightforward but nerve-racking, climbed on small holds mainly on its left side. FA Neil Macniven, 1960s.

◻ f. **B.N.I.** 5

Start at *Imposter Arête* and traverse diagonally across the orange slab, past a good central foothold, to the detached block on *Pendulum* and finish up this. A classic 60s highball thriller. FA Neil Macniven, 1960s.

◻ g. **B.N.I. Variation** 5+

After stepping right onto the slab, go straight up near the left arête, not using any holds on that. FA Brian Shields, 1960s.

◻ h. **B.N.I. Slab Direct** 5+

The most central challenge on the hanging slab. Start as for *B.N.I.* but from the good foothold move up to finish direct and centrally.

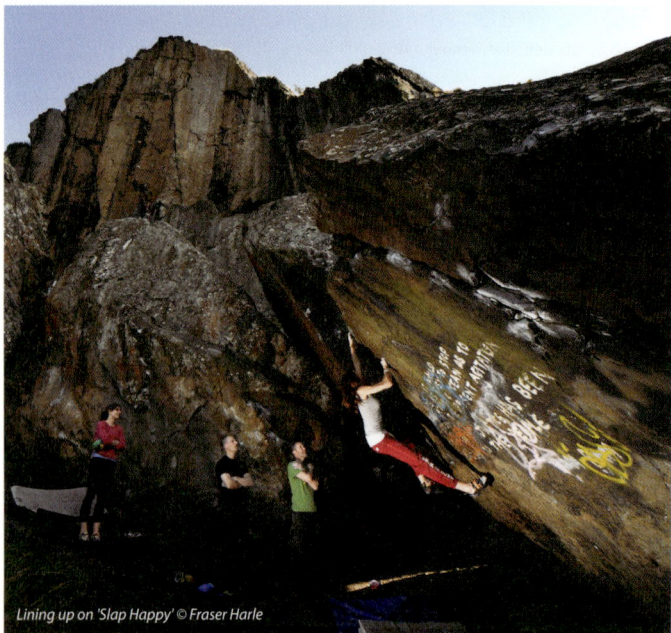

Lining up on 'Slap Happy' © Fraser Harle

20: PONGO FACE SECTOR

SECTOR 20: PONGO FACE

The classic leaning wall facing north-east over a gravel slope. Fingery, butch and technical.

☐ a. **Skint Knuckles** 4

The right-hand corner/groove in the cave tunnel. The original traversed in along the cave shelf utilizing a jammed sling on a chockstone. Modern ascents start using sidepulls left of the arête and layback up to mantle out right onto the ledges of the Pongo boulder. FA Brian Shields & Neil Macniven, 1964.

☐ a1. **Skint Sitter** 6c

An eliminate. Match the pinch hold on the arête, twist up to a left-hand three-fingertip sloper, then bounce into the long flake hold, finish up *Skint Knuckles*.

☐ a2. **Skint Cave Traverse** 6b+

The original problem without a sling round a chockstone! Start at the *Sanction* entrance split bloc at jugs, traverse right and drop down through slopey foot ledges to the pinch hold of the sit start then into *Skint Knuckles* via its wee crimp.

☐ b. **Slap Happy** 7a

The classic slopey campus problem on the left side of the face. It boasts the most polished foothold at Dumby. Climb dynamically through a high sloping right-hand crimp and a left-hand edge just under the lip, to gain a good hold over the lip. Rock over using the corner of the B.N.I. boulder. Depressingly, this has been done footless. Static is impressive enough. FA Andy Gallagher, 1993.

☐ b1. **Hap Slappy** 7b+

Reverse the *Slap Happy* starting sequence, taking the sloping crimp with your left hand. Crank to top with a dynamic throw or a high heel. FA Ben Pritchard, 2000.

☐ b2. **Happy Slap** 7c+

Slap Happy then descend to jug then just do *Hap Slappy*.

☐ b3. **Paedo Bikini** 7c

As for *Hap Slappy* but flick out right to the juggy nose of the boulder. Eliminate but a good problem. FA Will Atkinson.

☐ b4. **Slap Happy Dyno** 7c

Dyno from the first hold to the top, missing the middle crimp.

☐ c. **In Bloom** 7c+

Start matched at the arête left of *Slap Happy* and traverse right along the handrail via a crux drop-down move. If you can keep your feet on, continue along the rail and lunge to *Pongo* and finish up this. FA Dave MacLeod, 1998.

John Watson on 'Pongo'

Simon Smith before the crux dropdown of 'In Bloom'

❒ c1. **In Bloom Arête**   8a

Climb *In Bloom* to the *Pongo* crack. Continue right to the big flatty then to the arête and finish up this (*Andy's Arête*). Technical at the end.

❒ d. **Pongo**   7a

From the right side of the handrail, jump footless to the flange and then plant your feet. Continue up the powerful crack, with a crux slot move, to gain tenuous jugs at the top. Move left and rock up via holds on the nose feature, or continue leftwards to finish above *Slap Happy*. FA Gary Latter, 1980.

❒ d1. **Pongo Sit Start**   8a

The original method is aesthetically butch. Sit start at the ledge, gain the niche and contort through to a right-hand crimp or pinch on the rattly bloc. A dynamic press move to the base of the flange (off polished footholds) leads to a hard crossover to better holds. Finish up the original *Pongo* crack. FA Malcolm Smith, 1998.

❒ d2. **Pongo Stand**   7c

Static from the jammed bloc, pull feet onto polished ledges and crank through the crux moves. A jumping start drops this to 7b+.

❒ d3. **Pongo 'Cheat'**   7c

The 'Knuckle Sandwich' method that some find easier with tape, but some find desperate, depending on the width of your knuckles! Sit start at the ledge at the base of the crack, climb to the rattly bloc and knuckle-jam just above this with three right-hand fingers, then yard up to the flange and finish as for the original.

❒ d4. **Mr Tickle**   8a

Dyno from the mid-rail of *In Bloom* to the top of the V-shaped flatty of the *Pongo* crack. Supply your spotters with mouth guards. FA Will Atkinson, 2009.

❒ d5. **Mr Tickle Extension**   8a+

Climb *In Bloom* to the final frustrating dyno. FA Will Atkinson, 2009.

❒ d6. **Supersize Me**   8b

Sit start right of *Andy's Arête* at the big pocket on the slab, climb left into *Pongo Sit Start,* then reverse the handrail of *In Bloom* and finish up *Slap Happy* (where it is easy to fail on the redpoint). FA Malcolm Smith, 2005.

❒ d7. **Pongo via Arête**   7a+

Sit start as for *Pongo* and slap right to the arête. Move up this until it is possible to move leftwards to the top of the crack via a good long flat hold. Finish as for *Pongo*.

❒ e. **Andy's Arête**   7a

Sit start the far-right arête and climb it with laybacks on the overhanging side. Use holds on the leaning wall as well. FA Andy Gallagher, 1990s.

'Sorcerer's Slab'

21: PONGO SLABS SECTOR

❒ e1. **Buzz Saw** 7a+

Sit start at the shothole as for *Supersize Me* and finish up *Andy's Arête*. FA Neil Busby, 1990s.

❒ f. **The Dumbartoner** 7b

A fantastic excursion and hard to grade! No hanging around between boulders. *Pongo via Arête* > leftwards traverse of *Pongo* lip > down *Chahala* > *Off the Rails* > *Route Royale Wall Traverse* > *Presence* > *Home Rule High Traverse* > traverse to finish in the groove of *Head Butt*. FA Steve Richardson, c2005.

❒ g. **Rock Around the Bloc** 6c

Sit start at the base of *Pongo* and slap to an arête pinch, match this, then drop down the arête/slab on slopers for a couple of moves to rock right onto the slab via a distant pinch. Finish up the slab any way you wish. A higher version around the arête can also be done. FA John Watson, 2014.

❒ h. **Embrace the Rock** 7a+

Rock Around the Bloc, but keep low until you get to the pocket. Continue to the right and up the arête, using the slopers only, eliminating good holds to the right. FA Alexis Paulise, 2018.

❒ i. **Amalgamated** 7c

A further extension of *Consolidated*. Climb *Embrace the Rock* and drop into *Consolidated Extension*. FA Simon Smith, 2018.

SECTOR 21: PONGO SLABS

❒ a. **Sorcerer's Slab** 3

Pull on at the taper point of the slab, via a palm and slab crimp, by the shothole. Step onto the slab and travel steadily up and left, rising all the time near the left edge of the slab. Good holds appear towards the top. FA Neil Macniven & Brian Shields, 1960s.

❒ b. **Magic Wand** 3+

Start as for *Sorcerer's Slab* but go right a bit to a finger pocket, then aim straight up the centre via a blank section (crux, turned by kink to right, not escaping left). Continue straight to top on better holds. FA Neil Macniven & Brian Shields, 1960s.

❒ c. **Slant** 3

Pull on to the slab through the overhang via good crimps, gain a pocket on the slab, then step up through the overlap to gain the right edge of the slab, finish easily. Can be escaped right into *The Groove*. FA Neil Macniven & Brian Shields, 1960s.

❒ d. **Nemesis Left** 4+

Pull on slab holds just left of the nose then crank up right to jugs on the nose and rock left onto the slab, then take a small slab via an overlap to the right edge and step into the easy groove.

Beth Chalmers on 'Hard Cheddar'

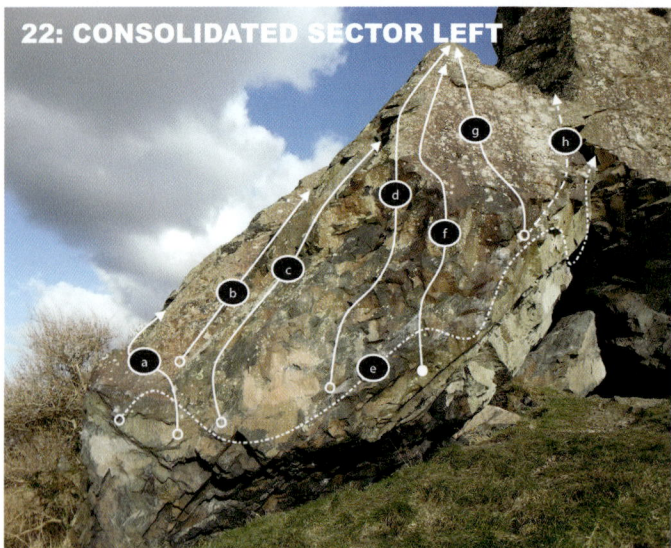

22: CONSOLIDATED SECTOR LEFT

❏ d1. **Shothole Sitter**   6a

Rising left to right traverse. Sit start at the taper left hand in the shothole and right hand in smaller shothole. Use toe hooks and a slopey left undercut to gain a press hold on the lip and cross over to finish up *Nemesis Left*.

SECTOR 22: CONSOLIDATED SECTOR

The undercut slabby west wall leading up a grass slope to the walkthrough cave.

❏ a. **Nemesis**   5

The nose at the base of the easy-angled groove is hard to surmount. From a poor right-hand finger lock crack, twist up to a good hold at the top of the nose and gain *The Groove*. FA Neil Macniven, 1963.

❏ a1. **Nemesis Sit Start Right**   6b+

Sit start at a large and hidden undercut low down to the right and make difficult moves leftwards to finish up the original problem.

❏ a2. **Nemesis Sit Start Direct**   6b

Sit start on the slabby side of the nose. Slap up slopey holds on the arête to a sloper on the nose then gain the hidden jugs above. No blocky pinch out right at the lip.

❏ a3. **EBGB**   6c

A forgotten classic and a higher precursor to *Consolidated*. Start at *Slant* and traverse right round the nose of *Nemesis*, then gain a standing position on the sloping ramp and traverse right round *Lunik* and *Cheddar* to finish up *Hard Cheddar*.

❏ b. **The Groove**   4+

Stand start just right of hanging groove. Use holds of *Narcosis* to bridge and stretch up left to a good jug which allows an easy pull into the easy groove.

❏ c. **Narcosis**   5

Blind climbing up the faceted wall right of *Nemesis*, directly above the large, hidden undercut. Use sidepulls and blunt holds to step on and use a high right crimp to step up into the slim hanging groove right of the bigger groove, finish up this.

❏ c1. **Narcosis Sit Start**   6a

Gain *Narcosis* from a sitting start at the large, hidden undercut.

❏ d. **Lunik**   4+

The scooped groove above the big flat slopers of *Consolidated*. Twist into the groove and climb the arête above right to the pointed apex. Technical.

❏ d1. **Lunik Sit Start**   6a

Sit start at the wide slopers in centre of the traverse and pull into the scooped groove, finish as for *Lunik*.

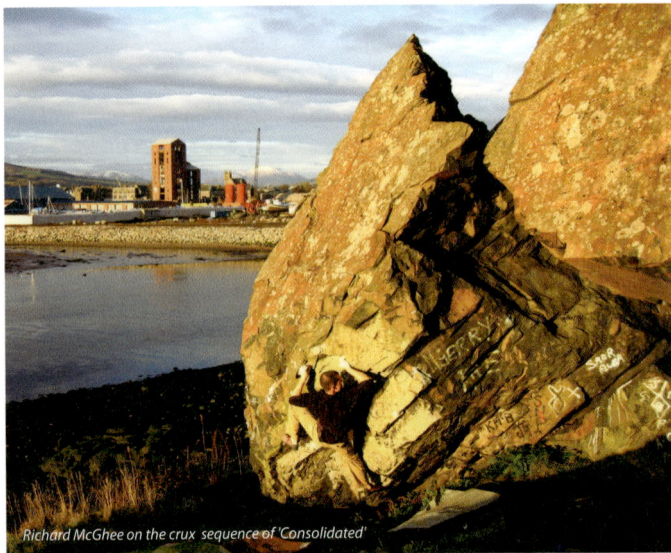

Richard McGhee on the crux sequence of 'Consolidated'

Pete Roy on the low section of 'Consolidated' © Fraser Harle

❑ e. **Consolidated** 7b+

The finest of the traverses at Dumby. From a stand start at sidepulls at the seaward nose just left of *Nemesis*, slap up to a polished crimp on the lip, take a small left-hand pinch and drop down low right to sloping press holds. Traverse low right on the big slopers to negotiate the blunt arête and niche under *Cheddar*. A crux sequence on white rock under the lip gains a big triangular hold, then slap up the hanging arête of *Juggie* to finish. Stays low and if the highish hold you're on seems a bit good it's likely out of bounds! FA Andy Gallagher, 1994.

❑ e1. **Consolidated Extension** 7c

Extend the traverse through the triangle to the descent hole, staying low and using a sidepull to lunge to the base of the ramp. FA Andy Gallagher, 1995.

❑ e2. **The '8b' Traverse** 7c+

Eliminate. As for *Consolidated Extension,* but once at the triangle use only a long thin crimp match just to the right to gain the slanting shelf. FA Dave Macleod 1998.

❑ f. **Rosie and Jim** 5+

Sit start at the blunt rib at the top of the grass slope, at a finger ledge under the slopers. Crank up via a right-hand crimp to a left-hand pinch to stretch up to a flat ledge left of the arête. Gain the slab and climb the left edge of this direct to the apex.

❑ g. **Cheddar** 4+

The undercut slab where the ground flattens out. From good incut holds at the base of the hanging slab, pull on and continue directly to the apex via a delicate move. FA (finishing left) Neil Macniven, 1963, FA (finishing right) Brian Shields, 1960s.

❑ h. **Hard Cheddar** 5+

A classic technical problem. Pull on as for *Cheddar* but immediately travel right along slopey flanges on the bottom lip of the slab to a hard move to gain a ledge above the arête of *Juggie*, then finish up the slab. FA Brian Shields, 1960s.

❑ h1. **Hard Cheddar Sit Start** 6a

Sit start the blunt arête, take the same moves as *Consolidated* but gain the jug on *Cheddar*, then finish right along the flanges of *Hard Cheddar*.

❑ h2. **Hard Cheddar Direct** 6a

Stand by the triangle hold, with a left-hand tan sidepull and a sharp right-hand undercut/sidepull above the triangle. Smear on to a blind left-hand lunge onto a slab pocket, then gain the slab direct without using jugs on *Juggie* arête.

❑ i. **Big Cheese** 7c

A one move power problem. Sit start at two very poor and wide pinches in the white groove under *Cheddar*, slap up into a left-facing sidepull crimp common to *Consolidated* and finish up *Hard Cheddar*. FA Dave MacLeod, 2003.

22: CONSOLIDATED SECTOR RIGHT

g
h
j
k
i
j5
j2
j1
h1

'The Jugs Don't Work'

☐ j. **Juggie** 4

The hanging arête just left of the descent route. Start at the big polished triangle hold. Slap up the arête via good incut holds and flanges out left, pull onto the slab.

☐ j1. **The Jugs Don't Work** 6b+

Sit start below the triangular hold, at a low left-hand crimp and a sharp right-hand V-hold. Slap to match the triangle, then finish up *Juggie*. FA John Watson, 2009.

☐ j2. **Jugs are For Mugs** 6b

Sit start further right, as for *Babybel*, at a right-hand sidepull/pinch. Gain the triangle, then finish up *Juggie*. FA Stuart Burns, 2016.

☐ j3. **Le Rustique** 6c

Sit start as for *The Jugs Don't Work* and transition left into *Hard Cheddar Direct* via the triangle hold and tan sidepulls. FA John Watson, 2014.

☐ j4. **Phoenix** 7a

Eliminate. Sit start low and right of the triangle (out). Gain the long crimp and throw a long lunge up to a triangle flattie right of *Juggie* and finish to jugs.

☐ j5. **Babybel** 6c+

From a low descent-hole sit, with a right foot on a low jug, use a right-hand sidepull/ pinch and left-hand crimp to slap left to the triangle. Swing left and reverse the *Consolidated* sequence to finish up *Cheddar*. A finish up *Hard Cheddar Direct* is 6c.

☐ k. **The Ramp** 5

Sit start the ramp at the tunnel and climb up left on polished layaways to a tricky exit onto the arête of *Juggie* to finish. Harder than it looks.

SECTOR 23: TRIPLETS

☐ a. **Short Sight** 3+

The crag side of the taller boulder of the Triplets facing *Consolidated*, following the right arête from a standing start.

☐ b. **Honesty** 6c+

Sit start the leaning wall in the cave at its left base, slap up via right arête to a poor left crimp on the wall, gain the high ledge on *Short Sight*.

☐ c. **Reducer Arête Right** 6a

Sit start the wee arête to the right.

☐ d. **Reducer** 7b

Eliminate. Sit start with hands on the dreadfully sloping ramp and power up to the sharp jugs direct, without the arêtes. For the strong fingered, two tiny crimps just left might be of use. Cold conditions essential! FA Dave MacLeod, 2001.

23: TRIPLETS BLOCS A-D

23: TRIPLETS BLOCS E-L

❑ e. **Reducer Arête Left**   5+

Sit start the wee arête to the left and head right on jugs to mantle out at the end.

❑ f. **Back Route**   2+

Ledges and polished jugs on the green back of the boulder facing the River Leven. Squeezed in, bridging allowed.

❑ g. **Descent Route**   1

The juggy ladder up the chimney side of the Ivy Bloc. Used as descent.

❑ h. **Rib Problem**   2

Pleasant rib and arête on the right of *The Long Reach*. Tricky high step at the top.

❑ i. **The Long Reach**   5+

The scooped slab facing out across the river. Use press holds and reach blindly up and left to a hidden hold on the slab and finish direct. A good technical problem.

❑ j. **Girdle Traverse**   5

Technical traverse of the scooped groove to finish round the three boulders more easily, finish up the *Rib Problem*. FA W. Bridges, 1960s.

❑ k. **Ivy Rib**   5+

Sit start at jugs and gain a sidepull on the right rib arête, then use slopey sidepulls to a hidden right niche on the wee slab. Left crimp on the slab and mantle.

❑ l. **Short Notice**   4

The little wall facing the River Leven. Use sidepulls on the right and left arêtes and step up to the top lip, mantle out.

SECTOR 24: SEA BOULDER

The isolated and partly tidal pillar bloc on the shore, with good landings and an easy but polished descent.

❑ a. **Curving Arête**   2+

The left lip bounding the descent groove of the north face, traversing right to gain the crack and jugs to step left onto the wee pillar.

❑ b. **Short Wall**   4

From chest-high sidepulls under the crack, pull on and cross left to crimps on the short wall, gain the lip of *Curving Arête*.

❑ c. **The Crack**   3

The diagonal, juggy crack to jugs at top of the wee pillar, climb up the higher left arête to step onto wee pillar left to finish.

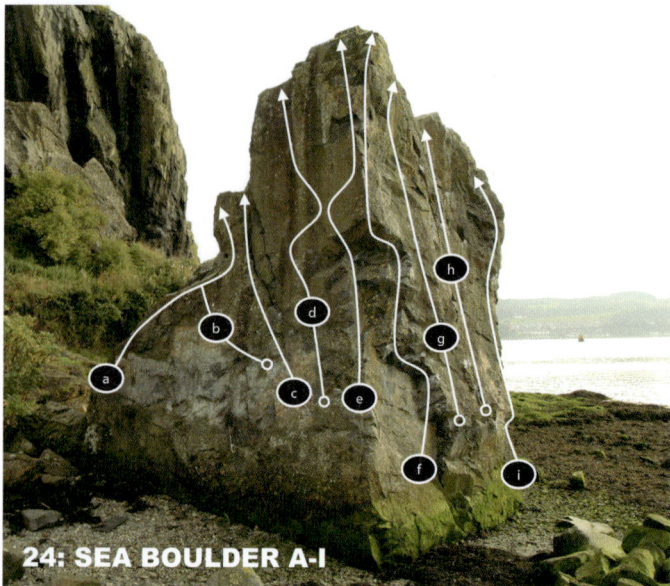

24: SEA BOULDER A-I

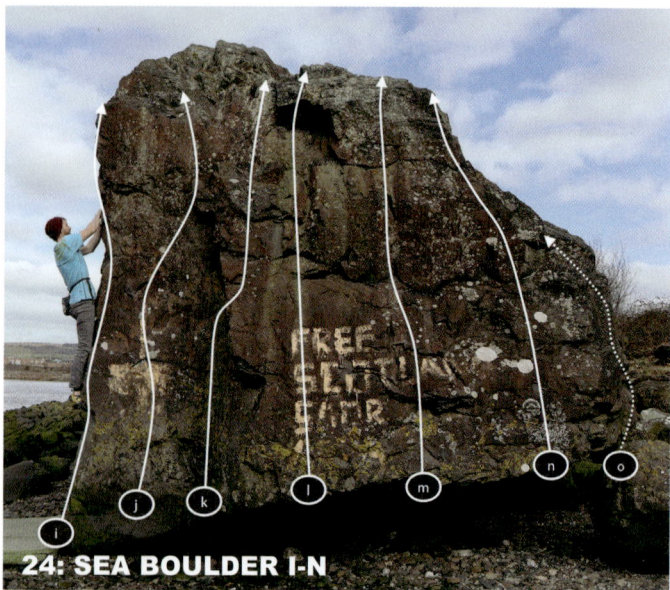

24: SEA BOULDER I-N

❏ d. **White Streak** 6b

The thin eliminate wall facing the stadium (no arêtes). Gain the crimps high on the wall via a triangular hold near the right arête. Lunge to the top left ledge (it's not a jug).

❏ e. **Steptoe Wall** 4

The tall narrow wall climbed using *Steptoe* arête and all holds on the left wall and short left arête, finish by pulling up on hidden jugs.

❏ f. **Steptoe** 3+

The arête climbed mainly on its right side, without the use of the old lump of tubular lead. FA Neil Macniven, 1960s.

❏ g. **Red Streak** 6a

The wall just right of *Steptoe*, no holds on *Chowbok* to the right nor the lump of lead! The crux is a technical step-up via a crimp to a higher crimp. Mantle out the top.

❏ h. **Chowbok** 3+

The cracked seaward wall in the centre to a pod and mantle at the top. FA Michael Connolly & Brian Shields, 1960s.

❏ i. **Erewhon** 4+

The super-polished right arête, using undercuts on the right wall and faith in feet! Jugs appear at half-height and the top is easier. FA Neil Macniven, early 1960s.

❏ j. **Tuesday Treat** 5

The narrow wall on the right side of *Erewhon*. FA Neil Macniven & J. Gardner, 1960s.

❏ j1. **Commercialism** 6a

Climb the narrow wall, eliminating the left arête and right corner. Pull on via a right sidepull to hard gaston moves to a high right niche hold and top out direct.

❏ k. **Commercial Route** 4

The corner just right of *Erewhon*, stepping onto the arête and right wall at half height. FA Brian Shields & Michael Connolly, 1960s.

❏ l. **Wednesday Wall** 4+

The slab and arête, using holds on both, to gain flatties and sidepulls above the *Free Scotland* graffiti, then finish up a vague groove.

❏ m. **Silver's Route** 3+

Sidepulls and smears up the slab and short wall. FA Michael 'Silver' Connolly, 1964.

❏ m1. **Silver's Route Sit Start** 6c+

Sit under the cave at opposing sidepulls and a heel-hook to a hard pull onto the slab. FA Mike Rudden, 2000.

Fred Carrick on 'Shattered Low Traverse'

25: EVERDRY WALLS SECTOR

❑ n. **Silver Rib** 3+

Pull onto the right arête/rib via smears and climb direct to top ledges.

❑ o. **Silver Arête** 6b

Sit start under the caved shore arête, squeezed in by the wee blocs, and campus up flatties to pull onto a standing position on the arête.

❑ p. **Gardner's Girdle** 4+

Traverse anti-clockwise low around the boulder from the descent groove, with the crux turning the *Erewhon* arête to the corner. FA Davie Gardner, 1960s.

SECTOR 25: EVERDRY WALLS

❑ a. **Shattered (High)** 6c+

Starts on the far right at the *Windjammer* corner and traverses to the far left to jugs on the arête of *Fever Pitch*. The best holds tend to be higher up, but anything is in.

❑ b. **Shattered (Low)** 7b

Eliminate. Traverse R-L from standing at the far right corner, under the sport route of *Appliance of Violence*. Crank through under *Longbow* corner (no high jugs) to the white arrow (no jug rest), then left to a drop-down at the wee shattered cave to finish at the left edge. The L-R version is possibly a little harder. FA Pete Roy, c1999.

❑ c. **Old Man's Corner** 6a

The chalky plethora of holds under the sports route have various eliminate possibilities from 6a to 7c. All finish at jump-off jugs.

❑ d. **Longbow Sit Start** 5+

Sit start in the dust by the rock plinth and climb the corner up the crack to ledges.

❑ e. **'This Place Is Shit'** 6a

Sit start at the wee cave and gain a right-hand pinch via a sharp rock-up, then use a left-hand hold up to left-facing smooth sidepulls. Egyptian to a high flat hold.

❑ f. **The Match** 6b

Sit start matched in a hidden undercut left of the wee cave, go right to match a sharp left-facing flange, crank and match higher sidepulls to the high flat finishing hold.

❑ f1. **The Slopers Problem** 6c+

Sit start the overhang at the low hidden undercut. Gain a good crimp with the left hand and use the right hand to cup a slopey hold on the shield. Cross through to the slopey sidepulls above to finish to the high right flattie. No big undercut out right.

❑ f2. **Liddell, Ha and Crombie** 6c+

From the undercut, climb straight up through a crimp to high jugs.

26: BLACK WALL SECTOR

Stewart Brown on the 'Sea Traverse'

SECTOR 26: BLACK WALL

❑ a. **Easy Crack** 3+

Layback the *Black Wall* crack on the left to mantle out onto ledges at top.

❑ b. **Mick T** 4+

Use a left-hand sidepull and right-hand finger lock under the niche to gain the high triangle hold and finish to ledges. A sit start makes this 6a.

❑ c. **The Niche Left** 5+

Sit start the wee pillar left of the niche and climb the left side of the crack higher up.

❑ d. **The Niche** 6a

Sit start the niche at a big flatty, gain pinches and then *The Black Crack* to finish.

❑ e. **The Black Crack** 5+

Traverse in from the corner jugs (left of the sports routes) and climb the diagonal crack over the niche to a juggy finish left.

❑ f. **Black Crack Circuit** 6a

Sit start at the right corner by the sport routes, up to finger ledges, then go hard left to *The Black Crack*. At the top of this, traverse left to descend *Easy Crack*, then a technical sequence low right through the niche leads back to the start. For each circuit, add a full grade until you drop off.

SECTOR 27: SEA WALLS

This south-west skirting board of sea-smoothed rock provides some excellent bouldering in the lower levels, though some finishes are highball and it's best to either downclimb and jump onto mats or traverse to easier ground and scramble descents. The approach is by scrambling down at low tide at the end of the grass platform under the black wall sports routes. The sea traverse is a classic outing and the tidal wall provides good straight-ups over gravel when the tide is out. The rock can be sea-polished but is compact and a delight to climb. If you are planning to climb on the tidal wall, please check tide times online for Dumbarton, as the tide comes in very quickly and can isolate you in the bay where the tidal wall sits. You can also escape right to the park. A large mat is useful to cover occasional rock spikes.

❑ **The Sea Traverse** 5

Traverse the low sea walls from below the right-most sport routes, there and back again, staying as low as possible on the best rock (often with hidden footholds). There are two distinctive crux sections, the first at the red slab area, then another on the steeper corners of the tidal wall (described below). This traverse is best done at high tide to focus the mind, but do not attempt it in choppy conditions, as the water can get quite deep in parts. At low tide, take care over rocky landings. The rock quality is excellent if a little polished in places. Great to finish your visit on a sunny evening.

SECTOR 27: SEA WALLS - TIDAL WALL

Descent

Sea Traverse

a b c d e f g h i j k l m n o

John Watson on 'Elevation' (left)

TIDAL WALL

❑ a. **Left Edge**   4
Take the left arête to a blank top, turned on right at half height for feet, descend b.

❑ b. **Descent Route**   1+
The stepped corner which is good for descents after traversing off other routes.

❑ c. **One-piece Puzzle**   5+
The slopey brown nose is taken direct from an incut. How to get off the ground?

❑ d. **Slab & Corner**   3
Step onto the slab delicately and trend right to a crack finish up left to ledges.

❑ e. **Corner Wall**   3
Step into the corner then up right onto ledges, then back left via crack holds.

❑ f. **Ledge Wall**   3
Climb corner then right onto the wall to a foot-ledge and trend left using crack.

❑ g. **Rib Climb**   4+
Climb the blunt rib to ledges and join *Ledge Wall* at half height.

❑ h. **Black Slab Crack**   4
Slab and corner crack to ledges. Swing right round arête at the top, traverse off right.

❑ i. **Flexation (left)**   4+
The steep wall from the corner but balance out right onto the wall and up to ledges.

❑ j. **Flexation (right)**   5
Step up off from a right sloping foot-ledge onto the arête foothold with the left foot.

❑ k. **The Groove**   3
Step awkwardly onto a ramp and move more easily up right via jugs.

❑ l. **Corner Crack**   2
Bridge up the corner using holds on both sides. Useful descent.

❑ m. **Snaking Cracks**   3
The scooped cracks right of the corner. Descend *Corner Crack*.

❑ n. **Red Rib**   4
Step up the brown/red blunt nose trending right, then back left to higher ledges.

❑ o. **Right-hand Groove**   2+
A steadier problem taking the right-hand groove to good jugs and a descent right.

Ben Litster on 'Silverback'

Thom Davies on 'Spam'

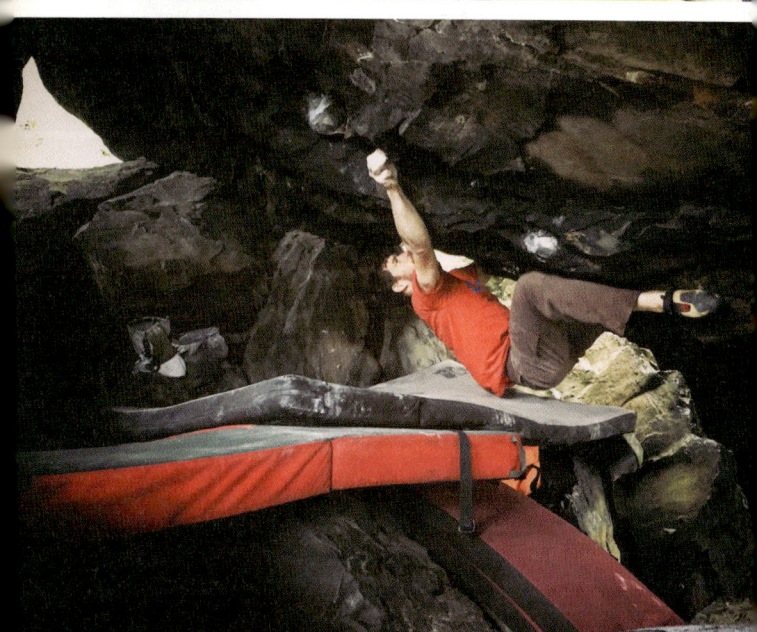

Alan Cassidy on 'Hokku' © Helen Cassidy

Malcolm Smith on 'Gutbuster'

Hamish Potokar on 'High Flyer' © Sam Scriven

BLOC TICKLIST

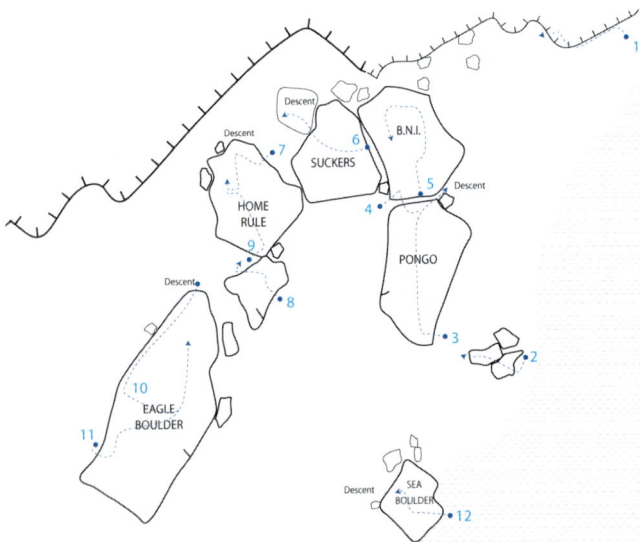

ORANGE CIRCUIT

Good composure is needed for this circuit, never hard but often polished! It is a traditional 'Font-style' alpine circuit which summits all the main boulders and sticks to rock as much as possible. Start at the base of the Pongo boulder's slabs. Grades in the Font 2 to 4 range.

- ❏ 1. **Sorcerer's Slab** > downclimb descent hole to:
- ❏ 2. **Cheddar Direct** > continue up next problem from ledge:
- ❏ 3. **Imposter Arête** > downclimb *Astronomy* to descent hole, to:
- ❏ 4. **Snooker Shelf** > start only, through gap to:
- ❏ 5. **Volpone** > over slab and downclimb easy rock to:
- ❏ 6. **The Beast** > downclimb *The Beast* and go under cave to:
- ❏ 7. **Friday's Fill** > down path to warm-up wall:
- ❏ 8. **Ungava** > cross to Eagle Boulder to:
- ❏ 9. **PTO** > downclimb descent and traverse low across slabs to:
- ❏ 10. **Left Direct** > downclimb descent and down to Sea Boulder:
- ❏ 11. **Chowbok** > down descent to:
- ❏ 12. **Steptoe** > and crack open a beer ...

BLUE CIRCUIT

This circuit is a little more technical and fingery, but good fun. Most of the problems are in the Font 3 to 5 ranges.

- ❏ 1. **Black Wall Crack** > walk across to Triplets boulders to:
- ❏ 2. **The Long Reach** > across grass to Pongo boulder:
- ❏ 3. **Nemesis** > up groove and down descent to:
- ❏ 4. **Chahala** > to ledges under B.N.I. prop slab:
- ❏ 5. **Deo Gratis** > downclimb *Astronomy* and descent hole to:
- ❏ 6. **Sucker's Slab** > up slab then down rock to step over to:
- ❏ 7. **The Beauty** > downclimb *The Beast* arête to warm-up wall:
- ❏ 8. **Friar's Mantle** > step right to Home Rule boulder:
- ❏ 9. **Presence** > downclimb *The Beast* and across to Eagle slabs:
- ❏ 10. **Centre Direct** > down descent route to:
- ❏ 11. **Zig Zag** > down descent to walk down to Sea Boulder:
- ❏ 12. **Erewhon** > and enjoy the view ...

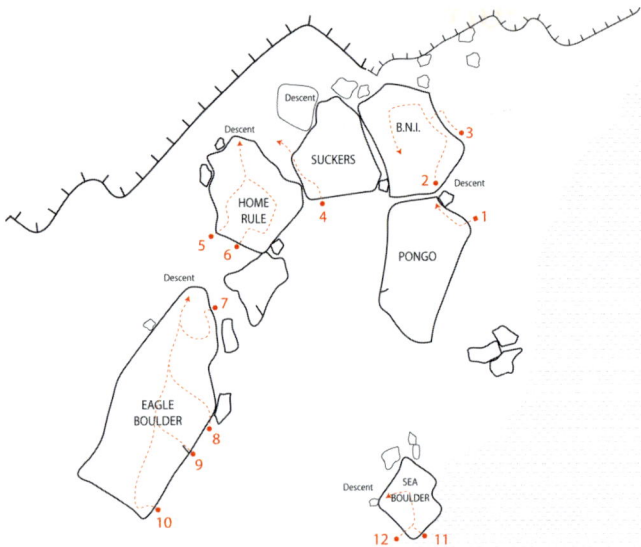

RED CIRCUIT

A fingery, technical, butch and bold circuit of problems from the classic 70s & 80s testpieces, some of which are getting polished, so care is needed. A full range of skills and commitment is needed to complete this circuit. Grades from Font 5 to 6b+.

❑ 1. **Hard Cheddar** > to ledges below B.N.I. slabs:
❑ 2. **B.N.I.** > downclimb *Astronomy* and descent hole:
❑ 3. **Good Nicks** > downclimb *Astronomy* or take the Jump!
❑ 4. **Toto** > round the back of the Home Rule boulder to:
❑ 5. **Mestizo** > downclimb *The Beast* to:
❑ 6. **Home Rule** > downclimb *The Beast* and cross to:
❑ 7. **Blue Meanie** > descent route of Eagle boulder to:
❑ 8. **2HB** > descent route of Eagle boulder to:
❑ 9. **Supinator** > descent route of Eagle boulder to:
❑ 10. **Gorilla** > descent route of Eagle boulder to:
❑ 11. **Red Streak** > downclimb Sea boulder then up to:
❑ 12. **White Streak** > enjoy the sunset!

BLACK CIRCUIT

For the gym-rats and local gurus. This suggested workout is more of a list of test pieces, ranging in difficulty from Font 6b+ to 7b+. Fingers of steel, hardened abs and a detailed memory for sequences is required to bust out this circuit. These are some of the classic test pieces of the modern era and a portfolio born of the 1990s.

❑ 1. **Pongo**
❑ 2. **Slap Happy**
❑ 3. **Toto Sit Start**
❑ 4. **Mestizo Sit Start**
❑ 5. **Mugsy Hanging Start**
❑ 6. **Home Rule Low Traverse**
❑ 7. **Physical Graffiti**
❑ 8. **Bust My Chops**
❑ 9. **Gorilla Hanging Start**
❑ 10. **Consolidated**
❑ 11. **The Shield**

'Niall McNair gaining the airmiles on 'Requiem' © Martin McKenna

'Gorilla Warfare' © Martin McKenna

Niall McNair recreating David Jones' iconic 1983 image of Cubby on 'Requiem' © Martin McKenna

Jess Gillespie on 'The Railings'

Brian Shields

Dave MacLeod

Stewart Brown

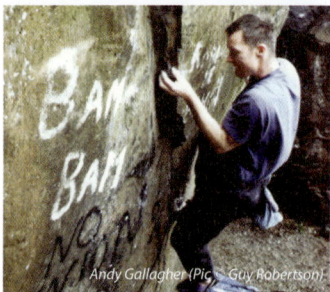

Andy Gallagher (Pic – Guy Robertson)

Steve Richardson

Malcolm Smith

ACKNOWLEDGEMENTS

Dumby is the sum of its constituent climbers, most of whom will never have met each other but all of whom have left their mark over the decades. Many climbers have invested vast amounts of their time in the intricacies of climbing at the Rock and the authors of this book would like to mention a few people in particular who have helped build the content of this guide, and some who have simply created a sporting heritage through their singular determination and vision.

Jon Shields, for letting us reproduce sections of his father Brian Shield's original handwritten guide from the early 60s, and for permission to reproduce rare photographs of the very first routes at Dumbarton Rock.

Frank Yeoman, **Ken Crocket**, **Ken Johnstone, Steve Richardson, Gary Latter**, **Andy Gallagher**, **Dave MacLeod, Malcolm Smith**: thanks go to them all for their dedication and many useful comments on the history of the ground-breaking routes and boulder problems at The Rock. In particular, we would like to thank **Stewart Brown** for his diligent copyediting and his contributions decanted from previous guides.

Thanks to all the photographers who contributed to the guide, capturing the atmosphere and exposure of climbing at Dumby, in particular: **Fraser Harle, Jonathan Bean, Gary Latter, Ian Campbell, Chris Houston, Tim Morozzo, Guy Robertson, Martin McKenna, Ry McHenry, Ken Crocket, Sam Scriven, Helen Cassidy** and **Beth Chalmers**.

BIBLIOGRAPHY

Whilst most of the current documentation of Dumbarton Rock is lodged on internet databases such as Dumby.info and UKC, the heritage of recording climbing at Dumbarton Rock goes back to the 1960s:

Guide to the Boulder Problems of Dumbarton Rock, Brian Shields, 1964
Glasgow Outcrops, Brian Shields et al, Highrange Sports, 1975
The Western Outcrops: A Climber's Guide, K.V. Crocket, Nevisport, 1975
Climbers' Guide to Central & Southern Scotland, ed. J. Handren, SMT, 1986
Lowland Outcrops, Tom Prentice and Grahame Nicoll, SMC, 1994
Lowland Outcrops, Tom Prentice et al, SMC, 2004
Dumbarton Rock, Stewart Brown, Stone Country Press, 2010
Dumby Bloc, John Watson, Stone Country Press, 2013

VISUAL INDEX TO DUMBARTON ROCK

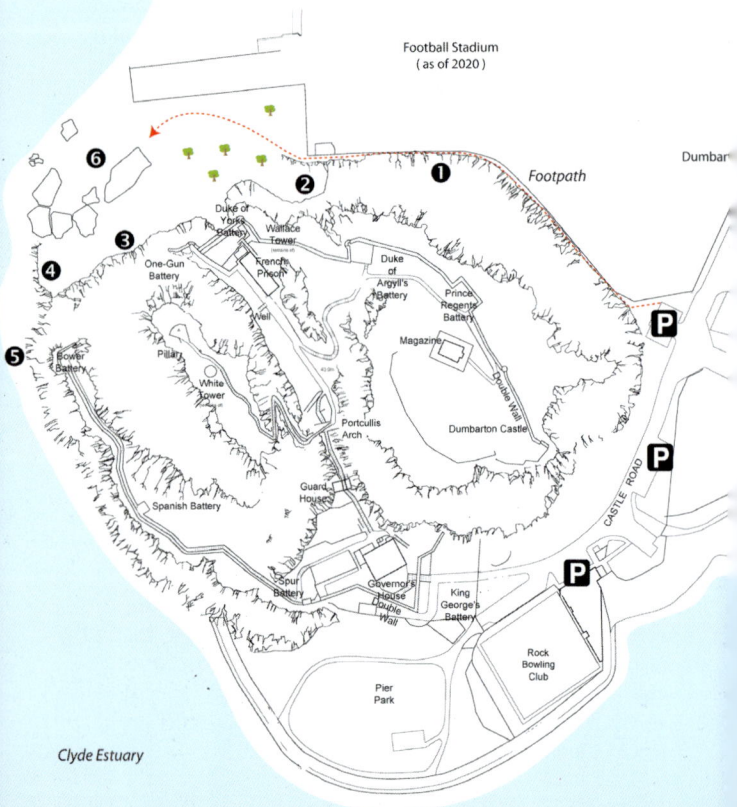

River Leven

Football Stadium
(as of 2020)

Footpath

Dumbar

Duke of Yorks Battery
Wallace Tower
French Prison
One-Gun Battery
Duke of Argyll's Battery
Prince Regents Battery
Magazine
Well
Pillar
White Tower
Bower Battery
Portcullis Arch
Dumbarton Castle
Double Wall
Guard House
Spanish Battery
Spur Battery
Governor's House
Double Wall
King George's Battery
Rock Bowling Club
Pier Park
Castle Road

Clyde Estuary